Creating Effective Sales and Marketing Relationships

Kenneth Le Meunier-FitzHugh
Senior Lecturer (Associate Professor) in Marketing
Norwich Business School
University of East Anglia
Norwich, UK

Leslie Caroline Le Meunier-FitzHugh
Lecturer (Assistant Professor) in International
Business Strategy
Norwich Business School
University of East Anglia
Norwich, UK

BEP BUSINESS EXPERT PRESS

Creating Effective Sales and Marketing Relationships
Copyright © Business Expert Press, LLC, 2015.

First published in 2015 by
Business Expert Press, LLC
222 East 46th Street, New York, NY 10017
www.businessexpertpress.com

ISBN-13: 978-1-60649-858-3 (paperback)
ISBN-13: 978-1-60649-859-0 (e-book)

Business Expert Press Selling and Sales Management Collection

Collection ISSN: 2161-8909 (print)
Collection ISSN: 2161-8917 (electronic)

Cover and interior design by S4Carlisle Publishing Services
Private Ltd., Chennai, India

First edition: 2015

10 9 8 7 6 5 4 3 2 1

Printed in the United States of America.

Creating Effective Sales and Marketing Relationships

Abstract

The aim of this book is to discuss how corporate sales and marketing functions can operate collaboratively. Although effective sales and marketing interactions are critical to achieving organizational goals, their practical working relationship is frequently described as being unsatisfactory. Sales and marketing have developing their own perceptions of what should be achieved and how it can be realized. Because of the differences that exist between sales and marketing, the exploration of the issues and possible solutions to the sales and marketing dilemma offers an exciting opportunity for practitioners and academics, both in the context of management, and training and development programs, to deliver superior customer value. We will explore how sales and marketing can become more competitive in the face of dynamic and borderless markets, where lead generation is less important than building long-term relationships with customers.

The book considers the follow areas related to the sales and marketing interface: How the crises in the sales and marketing interface became established. How alignment between sales and marketing can be achieved in lead generation. Consideration of the formal and informal methods of communication that can assist in establishing inter-functional collaboration. How collaboration between sales and marketing can improve customer relationships. The role of senior management in improving sales and marketing working relationships, and the optimization of the sales and marketing interface.

Keywords

Sales, Marketing, Conflict, Collaboration, Management, Communication, Lead Generation, Resources, Value Creation, and Competitive Advantage.

Contents

Diagrams

Case Studies

Introduction

The operation of the sales and marketing interface remains a critical and topical dilemma for executives. Sales and marketing functions have the capabilities required to assist the organization to adapt to rapidly changing environments through focusing on customer needs and the activities of competitors (Malshe 2010). To gain the maximum benefits for the organization, sales and marketing need to collaborate as this has been found to have the potential to affect the bottom line (Le Meunier-FitzHugh and Piercy 2007). Sales and marketing functions also have the common goals of understanding customer needs and solving customers' problems in a way that is superior to their competitors. Consequently, to achieve these and other common goals, it is necessary for sales and marketing to collaborate and interact effectively. However, they are frequently managed as individual functions with their own objectives, behaviors, and culture which may impede collaboration. In spite of decades of lip service to the importance of internal integration, achieving effective sales and marketing relationships has proved elusive for many organizations.

Why Improve the Sales and Marketing Interface?

Although effective sales and marketing interactions are critical to achieving organizational goals, their practical working relationship is frequently described as being unsatisfactory (Aberdeen Group 2002). Sales and marketing are often managed as individual functions, which have led to each group developing their own perceptions of what should be achieved and how it can be realized, as well as their individual perceptions they have developed, very different skill sets, and behaviors. These characteristics emphasize some of the issues that exist in the sales and marketing interface. Research has found some very destructive sales and marketing behaviors, such as withholding information, distrust, creating obstructions to decision making, and opportunistic actions (Kotler, Rackham, and Krishnaswamy 2006). The result of these behaviors leads to a reduction in performance, dissatisfaction, and increased tension between the two groups. Because of the differences that exist between sales and marketing, the exploration of the issues and possible solutions to the sales and marketing dilemma offers an exciting opportunity for practitioners and academics, both in the context of management, and training and development programs, to deliver superior customer value.

While it is understood that marketing is the anchor of sales (Capon 2011), it is sales that delivers the orders that the organization relies on to succeed. Marketing can lay the foundation for sales success through communications with the market place, creating and communicating brand values and providing promotional materials. In a real sense, marketing actions should dovetail with sales so that they can deliver the value that the market is demanding. It is necessary then, for sales to have a clear and unambiguous idea of what marketing is trying to achieve and how they intend to achieve it. This understanding should help to guide the sales manager's decision-making process. Sales should also be able to engage with marketing so that they feed information into marketing decision-making processes and aid their market comprehension. The sales force is an ideal position to provide this understanding of the market. Each manager should not be shy in pushing their counterpart to deliver on their jointly conceptualized customer value and this can only be achieved when sales have a deep understanding of marketing, and marketing really appreciates what sales is trying to achieve. "After all, marketing and sales are in the competitive battle together." (Capon 2011, 594)

Objectives

The objectives of this book are to consider the touch-points that exist between the sales and marketing functions to identify how they can be leveraged to the organization's advantage, and to recommend strategies to overcome the barriers that have developed over time between the two groups. This should result in a number of benefits for sales and marketing functions, as well as for the organization as a whole. Collaborating sales and marketing functions should allow the full development of marketing ideas, which should lead to sales receiving promotional materials that are relevant and up to date, and the customers will receive a coherent message that will result in the creation of customer value. The alignment of sales and marketing activities should result efficiencies in operation. The aim is to create a situation where there is a dynamic interaction or synergy between the two functional areas that results in greater value for the organization than they can create independently (Rouzies et al 2005). To achieve these objectives we shall first review the existing crises in the working relationship between sales and marketing, and then consider how to optimize working relationships through overcoming organizational and structural barriers. We shall also review how to improve of sales and marketing collaboration, its benefits and its impact on the organization.

Structure

This book consists of seven chapters considering the following:

Chapter 1: *The Sales and Marketing Interface*—reviews why the sales and marketing interface has recently come into focus as requiring management attention. The benefits of an effective and collaborative sales and marketing function are reviewed and the background to research into this interface is summarized.

Chapter 2: *Crises in the Sales and Marketing Interface*—considers some of the barriers to integrating sales and marketing activities. The differences between functional and dysfunctional conflict are examined, and how cultural, organizational, and infrastructural barriers may become established.

Chapter 3: *Alignment and Effective Working Relationships in Lead Generation*—explores how some of the structural and organizational barriers to collaborative sales and marketing may be overcome through alignment of processes. The chapter reviews the key process of lead generation, and how it may be aligned to reduce friction.

Chapter 4: *How should Sales and Marketing Communicate?*—considers how communication (dialogue) between sales and marketing can be created and leveraged to improve the alignment between sales and marketing functions.

Chapter 5: *The Role of Sales and Marketing in Customer Relationships*—reviews the importance of building long-term relationships with the customer and the relevance of trust, both inter-personal and inter-organizational, is explored. Finally, the concept value and how value may be co-created with sales and marketing is considered.

Chapter 6: *Managing the Sales and Marketing Interface*—outlines the importance of senior management's role in communicating their attitude to collaboration and reviews how managers may facilitate collaboration in the sales and marketing interface through employing a number of integrative activities (e.g., cross-functional teams, cross-functional meetings and planning, joint training, job rotation, and joint rewards).

Chapter 7: *Optimizing the Sales and Marketing Interface*—this final chapter considers how structure and location may influence the working relationship between sales and marketing, and considers other possible solutions to improving the interface.

Who Is this Book for?

We believe that this book will be a valuable resource to all students of management, but is especially relevant to MBA and executive MBA students with an interest in business-to-business marketing, as well as students studying for qualifications in sales and marketing (undergraduate and postgraduate) around the world. Further, the text should be attractive to managers with an interest in the management of sales and marketing and how it impacts on the organization.

Finally

We hope that you will enjoy your journey through the challenges and issues that exist between sales and marketing. We do not offer finite solutions, but present a range of possible options and links, that should enable managers to evaluate their current situation and develop the most suitable structure and processes for their organization.

Kenneth Le Meunier-FitzHugh and
Leslie Caroline Le Meunier-FitzHugh, 2015

CHAPTER 1

The Sales and Marketing Interface

Introduction

The relationship between sales and marketing personnel has presented a number of challenges for many organizations. Even organizations that have integrated sales and marketing activities have experienced tensions. Over the past few years there have been many and varied debates around this topic, but still stories continue about poor support from marketing and misuse of marketing materials by sales. However, whichever side of the debate you are on there are a number of views to consider, and no one has yet come up with the ultimate solution.

Creating Customer Value

Marketing is concerned with the process of "creating, communicating and delivering value to customers and for managing customer relationships in ways that benefit the organization and its stakeholders" (American Marketing Association 2004). This definition highlights the importance of customer value to organizational success. It also confirms the central role that customer relationships play in creating sales for the organization. As salespeople are those members of the organization who most frequently communicate directly with customers, customer relationships are usually managed through this function. The division between the sales and marketing functions is therefore evident even in the 2004 definition of marketing by the American Marketing Association. Sales and marketing have different competences and are frequently structured and managed separately in larger organizations (Piercy 2006). Consequently, although sales and marketing functions have the same overall goal of creating added value for their customers, thereby generating increased sales and profit for the organization, they still have their own objectives, behaviors, and culture. Marketing is generally more concerned with longer-term strategic objectives related to communicating value, while sales is more concerned on shorter-term sales objectives that relate to meeting customer needs (Ernst, Hoyer, and Rubsaamen 2010). Both functions, however, are critical parts of the customer value chain that needs to operate in a seamless manner.

The customer value chain is a way of thinking about how an organization is able to outperform its competitors and secure sales. This value chain is based around the core business processes of marketing and how well these activities are coordinated (Hammer and Champy 1993; Porter 1980). Five core processes in the creation of customer value are directly relevant to the sales and marketing relationship.

- Market Sensing—this relates to all the activities that are in management of market information, including the collection of data, analysis to identify new insights into the market, and the dissemination of market information to all parts of the organization. Consequently, sales and marketing have to share information in an integrated fashion to provide a complete picture of the market.
- New Offering Realization—this is concerned with the research and development of new products. Sales and marketing should be involved in the concept stage as well as the implementation stage of new product development (Ernst, Hoyer, and Rubsaamen 2010), and therefore they will need to communicate together on market changes and customer needs.
- Customer Acquisition—this is a key area in which sales and marketing are required to interact and cooperate. Customer acquisition relates to targeting and engaging new customers and understanding their needs, which cannot be achieved individually.

- Customer-Relationship Management—the customer-relationship process has developed and increased in importance over the past few years, as customer needs have become more complex and customer retention has become more difficult (Piercy, Cravens, and Lane 2007). While sales have traditionally been responsible for customer relationships, the development of the Internet has meant that there is more direct contact between the customer and marketing. Effective customer relationships are therefore requiring greater internal communication and interaction than previously was required.
- Fulfillment Management—this refers to the process that fulfills the customer's needs that is, receiving orders, shipping items, and collecting payment. Although this does not directly relate to the sales and marketing relationship, it does require the information on customer requirements to be effectively communicated to the supply chain.

The result of reviewing the effects of the sales and marketing interface on these key processes in the customer value chain highlights why this interface has gain so much recent management attention. Cross-functional sales and marketing cooperation is essential to delivering excellence in the customer-relationship management that leads to customer satisfaction (Guenzi and Troilo 2007). As market places become more competitive, organizations are increasingly reliant on the sales from fewer customers (Capon 2011). Consequently, deep insights into these customers' needs at both domestic and global levels are required for success. Focusing on offering superior customer value and quality customer relationships through integrated sales and marketing functions will assist the organization to grow and create competitive advantage.

Operation of the Sales and Marketing Interface

So what are the problems with the sales and marketing interface? Friction between sales and marketing has been generated over time and can be caused by a number of factors including:—the allocation of resources and how these resources are used, conflicting goals set by senior management, misunderstanding of each roles and the lack of high quality interaction. On the whole marketing personnel and sales personnel have good personal working relationships, but it is the demand of their roles and how these roles interrelate, which are causing difficulties and impacting on customer value. A disconnect between sales and marketing functions that has been observed in many organizations, in both business-to-consumer (B2C) and business-to-business (B2B) organizations. Marketing efforts are usually directed at supporting sales in finding new customers, but there are a lot of lost and dormant leads in most organizations. The Aberdeen Group (2002, 1) found that

> *"As much as 80% of marketing expenditure on lead generation and sales collateral are wasted—ignored as irrelevant and unhelpful by sales."*

There are many examples of this lack of collaboration between sales and marketing. One example from our own experience is of a marketing department producing materials specifically for a new product launch. Although this material was produced in full consultation with marketing teams from each territory, the sales teams were not fully engaged with the process. In some territories the sales terms felt that the specifications were not presented correctly, in others the data sheets provided were insufficient, and in some the materials produced were not suitable at all. The marketing departments from each territory had apparently not met/considered the opinions of their sales teams during the consultation. Developing marketing materials that include both sales and marketing perspectives is just a small example of how sales and marketing should work together as salespeople have insights into customers' needs and activities of competitors that were not always being integrated into marketing's thinking, and marketing have an overview

Diagram 1 Sales and Marketing Alignment

of the market and brand values that are not always being shared with sales (see Diagram 1).

Observing this disconnect has led to nearly 12 years of personal research into how to optimize sales and marketing operations across organizations, markets, country boundaries, and cultures. The topic continues to present challenges, as it is very hard to achieve sales and marketing collaboration overnight. This has to do with differences that exist between the two groups in function, objectives, strategies, history, and skill sets. Additionally, there are a number of conditions that exist, which need to be identified before discussing the sales and marketing interface any further.

1. Goal setting by senior management. It has been frequently found that sales and marketing have different time horizons. Sales usually have shorter-term targets, often based around monthly and quarterly quotas. Recording the number of calls made and number of presentations given may be measures of achievement and can be used in addition to actual sales achieved. Sales staff may also be rewarded on a commission based on actual sales, rather than for business development. On the other hand marketing often have longer-term goals regarding brand value, leads generated, and market visibility. Marketing personnel are usually rewarded through salaries and bonuses based on business success, rather than achieving specific sales targets. More recently organizations have been moving toward measuring marketing activities in terms of return on investment and sales success.

2. The background of sales and marketing personnel have traditionally differed as, to date, there has been a disparity in their training. Marketing personnel are often graduates of bespoke marketing courses from leading schools and universities around the world. Whereas, sales personnel, although graduates, often received their sales training whilst in post. This is slowly changing with specialist graduate courses in sales being developed, but there are still very few of these outside the U.S. It could be argued that the differences in education and training of sales and marketing personnel develops two different skill sets that are designed to meet the demands of their roles, but this may also create very different perspectives between the two

groups. This difference may be exacerbated by the appointment of sales managers from the ranks of the sales team, often the best sales person, (see Sales Managers, Marketing's best example of the Peter Principle, Anderson, Dubinsky, and Mehta 1999) rather than someone with more general managerial experience.

3. Lead generation and handover have always been thorny subjects between sales and marketing. The famous film "Glengarry, Glen Ross" (1992) has epitomized the relationship between sales leads and sales success (not necessarily in a good way, but one that has forever linked sales success to good lead generation). With the development of sales automation there seems to be an even bigger move toward the principle role of marketing as the lead generator, which they then hand on to sales. Where this falls down is that sales leads may not be qualified prior to handover, and salespeople feel that they spend a great deal of time chasing leads that are unproductive or nonexistent. This creates confrontation between sales and marketing staff, and sales feel that the only solution is to generate their own leads, as marketing does not understand their needs and requirements of the job.

4. Structure and location of sales and marketing personnel may also be a significant factor in the relationship between the two groups. Sales personnel are usually field based, with little time to spend in the office. This creates two issues, a) "out of sight is out of mind," and b) "we never know what our salespeople are doing." This can lead to more and more control mechanisms being employed to measure and motivate sales activities. Conversely, marketing staff are frequently office based, sometimes centrally based, and are therefore more likely to be included in management discussions and decision making. These location realities may contribute to the problem of creating meaningful communication and dialogue between sales and marketing staff.

The first critical step to improving the sales and marketing interface is to create an environment that allows collaboration and alignment across sales and marketing activities. To achieve this it is necessary to identify the role and focus of sales and marketing activities. Simply put, marketing's role is to create attention for the organization's offers in the market place and to create a landscape where sales can achieve their objectives. The sales role is to create links to customers so that they can meet their needs with the sales offer. Although they have different imperatives, we will argue that success is dependent on collaborating for mutual benefit.

Collaboration Versus Integration

Over the past few years there have been a number of calls for the integration of sales and marketing activities. We argue that "integration" would imply the bringing together of sales and marketing activities into a single department. For many organizations this would be impractical, if not impossible, due to the size of sales and marketing teams and the diverse nature of the organization. The term collaboration has been described as working together, indicating the need to build understanding between two different entities or groups. Collaboration has also been defined as creating collective goals, mutual understanding, sharing resources and creating an esprit de corps, which would all impact positively on business outcomes (Kahn 1996; Le Meunier-FitzHugh and Piercy 2007). Collaboration should lead to an efficient use of resources. Another term that has been growing in importance when addressing the sales and marketing interface is alignment. Alignment is concerned with the linear or orderly arrangement of processes (or items) so that there is a logical flow. Alignment is also about the correct positioning of something for efficient performance. Consequently, alignment embodies the concept of bringing something together in the most beneficial manner to achieve an objective. The use of the terms integration, alignment, and collaboration have been relatively interchangeable when talking about the sales and marketing interface, but we would suggest that collaboration, rather than alignment or integration, is the most appropriate term, because we feel that collaboration includes alignment, with the addition of cooperation, joint planning, and mutual support without the physical union that is so difficult to achieve with the diverse activities of these two functions. However, we should note that collaboration could not be entirely achieved without some physical interaction so that activities can be aligned to achieve common goals (see Diagram 2).

Consequently to the question—should you amalgamate sales and marketing into a single department? The answer is not necessarily. What

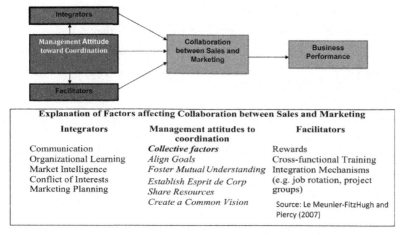

Diagram 2 *Creating Collaboration between Sales and Marketing*

is required are the processes and structures that support collaboration between sales and marketing departments to improve effectiveness in creating greater customer value and increasing sales.

The Changing Role of Sales

Sales have probably seen more changes in the last 10 years than they have done in the previous 50 years. They are operating in a more challenging environment than ever before. Sales practices are being forced to change and are moving away from a tactical focus to a more strategic one. Although traditionally sales personnel have focused on pushing products and services into the market (Moncrief and Marshall 2005; Weitz and Bradford 1999), the increasing complexity of the sales environment requires the salespeople to become more flexible and sensitive to the needs of their customers (Tuli, Kohli, and Bharadwaj 2007). The power has shifted from the seller to the buyer and the focus has moved from the product alone to a combination of both product and service. Managing customer expectations and building relationships is being driven by a concentration of buyers, hyper competition, new distribution channels, and longer sales cycles.

Organizations are experiencing longer sales cycles. This is being driven by a combination of more people in the decision-making process and because buyers require more information before making decisions, especially with complex products and services. Considerable product and service information is available through the Internet, so that buying departments carry out their own evaluation of offers being made to them before meeting the sales team or contacting the organization. Customers are demanding more from organizations in terms of presentation and marketing collateral. Consequently, salespeople are required to provide an integrated offer in line with their brand and organizational values. Further there is a move away from transactional to relationship selling. There is a greater requirement to hold and develop existing customers. To respond to the more tailored approach necessary to build customer relationships the sales team needs to be able to provide specific customer groups with multiple solutions (Homburg, Workman, and Jensen 2000; Piercy, Cravens, and Lane 2007). Salespeople are now taking the lead in relationship management, but this has to be supported by marketing messages through traditional media and more importantly through the web and social media.

Salespeople are facing customers and consumers who have much more information available and who are contacting the organization through a number of channels. As customers become more demanding, it is common to find sales organizations under intense pressure to meet elevated expectations (Ingram, Schwepker, and Hutson 1992). Salespeople need to upskill and develop integrated, multiple solutions for their customer groups, especially in high value goods and services (Lian and Laing 2006; Sheth and Sharma 2008). In other words salespeople are becoming business partners and have to understand customer data, analytics, and skills that are more traditionally associated with general management. This makes it an imperative for sales and marketing to work together strategically to provide solutions to customers, build trust and long-lasting relationships with both the customers and each other.

Case Study 1

An Illustration of How Roles of Sales and Marketing Are Changing

There has been much recent discussion about the changing nature of sales. These changes have never been more apparent than in the way that organizations are managing accounts. A few years ago a Unilever sales representatives would have serviced every small grocery store with dedicated, regional sales representatives. These grocery stores are now supplied through wholesalers and Unilever will usually only directly service large accounts. The reason for this has been put down to increasing costs (with the sales call costing anything up to $500 just to walk through the door) and the need for large accounts to be managed for long-term value, rather than for transactional sales. The growth of key accounts (very large customers operating nationally and globally) has led to the integration of systems and processes between the manufacturer and key account to more fully meet the customers' needs.

The combined drivers of rising costs and changing nature of selling has meant that the internal integration of activities, in particular between sales and marketing, is becoming more critical to success. Further, sales executives can no longer afford to operate as a lone wolf. The result is that manufactures employ smaller teams of specialist representatives who have higher skill levels that customize their offers to the larger customers, and integrate the competences of the organization with the requirements of the customer. Small grocery outlets still receive calls from sales representatives, but they are more likely to be representing a complete catalogue range on behalf of the wholesaler. These sales people have a different skill set in that they configure the offers to meet the local needs and build closer relationships with the outlet managers. The result is the professionalization and up-skilling of the field sales representative into relationship managers, who interact with both internal and external contacts.

The role of marketing is also changing due to the development of a global market place, the growth of social media and changing customer's types. This has lead to a divergence in focus for marketers. They have to take a broad view of the market and take responsibility for national and international marketing campaigns, market research and brand management. Marketers also have to support the changes that have occurred in sales through their marketing activities. It should not be forgotten that marketing's role is to support the sales operation in meeting customers' needs, whether they are selling a consumer or an industrial product, or selling direct to the end user or through intermediaries. Sometimes this is where the breakdown of the sales and marketing relationship occurs. It is possible for marketing to fail to appreciate their responsibility to support the individual sales representative and the customer, while they are trying to build the brand as a whole. With marketing worrying about the big picture they are ignoring the smaller, incremental changes that are required in the offer, to their detriment.

The Changing Role of Marketing

The markets today are becoming more complex. There is a need for marketing to play a more critical role in understanding customer relationships, which requires the use of all the resources available in a more consistent manner. This is being driven by the growing use of social media and more market knowledge being developed through direct customer interactions. Customers qualify the organizations' ability to provide the goods and services required before contacting the organization. Consequently, marketing are developing white papers, case studies, and briefing documents to support and verify their offerings to the market before any interaction takes place. Additionally, to generate leads, marketing need to understand the use of websites and how these are crucial to lead generation as well as developing and retaining existing customers.

Sales and marketing jointly should also take the lead on developing market information. This requires the collection, analysis, storage, and dissemination of market information to all parts of the organization. Sales and marketing should be collaborating in the collection and dissemination of this information. Market information should assist with working with other departments in the development of new products and offers. Marketing have a role to play in understanding and communicating future trends to the organization, as well as the customer. Finally, sales and marketing operations are being affected by e-marketing and the web. As more sales come through the web, marketing people have to adopt sales skills and handle transactional sales, and even start relationships with customers. There is a need to engage with customers, so marketing can no longer be detached from the customer experience.

Summary

In response to the increasingly dynamic markets, both domestically and globally, organizations are being forced to be more innovative and integrated to gain and retain market share. Within this context, the activities of the organizations' sales and marketing functions are inextricably linked, because an excellent, well-researched marketing strategy is altogether useless unless it is supported by a well-designed and executed, integrated sales strategy (Capon 2011). Managers to overcome a number of physical and psychological barriers that may prevent these functions from achieving their full potential. To achieve an integrated marketing and sales strategy requires the following:

- Organizations need to work to align sales and marketing so that they can create the value that customers are looking for from organizations in the twenty-first century.
- To be aware of the changing roles of sales and marketing in today's environment.
- Improving the sales and marketing interface can affect the bottom-line performance.

The next chapter will review these barriers in greater depth.

Key Points

1. Sales and marketing activities are inextricably linked, but they are managed in an individual manner that may lead to reductions in effectiveness.
2. The sales and marketing interface conceals complex relationship that is frequently invisible to senior management.
3. Complexities are created by conflicting short and long-term goal horizons set to sales and marketing, differing backgrounds, a dependent interrelationship, and location.
4. We highlight the importance/benefits of creating collaboration between sales and marketing departments.
5. The role of both sales and marketing functions is changing rapidly, driven by a new market environment.

CHAPTER 2

Crises in Working Relationships between Sales and Marketing

Introduction

There are a number of barriers to the successful operation of the sales and marketing interface. These have been summarized as problems generated as marketing has become separated from the sales function. Friction can be caused by a number of factors including, the allocation of resources and how these resources are used, conflicting goals set by senior management, misunderstanding of each others' roles, and the lack of high quality interaction. This chapter considers some of these barriers in greater depth.

Growth of Conflict

Conflict is perhaps not the right word to categorize the sales and marketing relationship because most sales and marketing staff would say that they work well with their opposite number inside the organization. This is true on balance, but the key issue is that sales and marketing operations are not always actively collaborating. This lack of coordination or alignment of activities can prevent additional value being created for the customer, and leads to an increase in irritating niggles in interdepartmental relations. Lorge (1999) and Shapiro (2002) were some of the early identifiers of the issues found between sales and marketing, but it was the key article in the Harvard Business Review by Kotler, Rackham, and Krishnaswamy (2006), which really brought matters into focus, supported by the more structured investigations by the Aberdeen Group (2002). So is there conflict between sales and marketing staff? Yes, it appears that there is. There are a plethora of apocryphal stories, and many supporting quotes to support this position, for instance:

> *"Marketing is locked in the Ivory Tower. They don't have a clue that customers really want."* (Shapiro 2002, 1)

> *"Salespeople are too busy to share their experiences, ideas, and insights."* (Kotler, Rackham, and Krishnaswamy 2006, 75)

> *"Salespeople ignore corporate branding and positioning and just do their own thing."* (Aberdeen Group 2002, 1)

> *"We [sales] make money and they [marketing] spend it."* (Shapiro 2002, 1)

> *"We generate leads and create sales support materials that get ignored."* (Aberdeen Group 2002, 1)

> *"Sales are slow to learn about new products—getting them up to speed takes forever."* (Aberdeen Group 2002, 1)

> *"Marketing wouldn't know a qualified lead if it tripped on one"* (Aberdeen Group 2002, 1).

These comments appear to rotate around the need for marketing to support sales with leads and marketing materials, and for sales to provide market information in good time and in useable form. This interdependence is at the heart of the problem. Interdependence relies on trust. Trust that the other party will perform their part of the operation.

> *"There's a significant lack of trust in the tools that marketing departments provide to their sales teams… marketing feels that they're often ignored or that their efforts are unappreciated."* (Krol 2003, 1)

Sales and marketing operate over a continuum of activities focused on the customer, but the responsibility for these activities moves from marketing to sales as they move closer to the customer (Cespedes 1995). How and when this responsibility changes is a source of uncertainty. Consequently, the divide between sales and marketing functions has been expanded by failing to adopt agreed definitions of role and function, failure to deploy effective processes and workflows between the two groups, and a lack of common measures of success (Aberdeen Group 2010). The result may be conflict.

There continues to be some argument over the nature of conflict between functional groups. Is it detrimental or beneficial to efficiency and performance? Two distinct types of conflict have been identified in cross-functional relationships (Barclay 1991; De Dreu and Weingart 2003):

1. Dysfunctional conflict, which results in negative outcomes and poor performance.
2. Functional conflict, which results in more positive outcomes in terms of efficiency driven by healthy competition and an open exchange of ideas and views.

The distinction between functional and dysfunctional conflict should be seen as separate concepts with their own consequences. Dysfunctional conflict is the more negative form and is associated with withholding information, distrust and hostility, opportunistic behavior, impeding decision-making, and low levels of cooperation. The result may be a reduction in performance, dissatisfaction and little value. It is this dysfunctional conflict of which the sales and marketing interface should be wary. Functional conflict on the other hand may bring benefits to the organization and the sales and marketing relationship as it allows the personnel to challenge preconceived ideas, express their opinions, and engage in open discussion. The benefit of functional conflict is that it reduces silo thinking and opens the decision-making process up to new possibilities (Tjosvold 1988). Management can affect which type of conflict is dominant through how they manage sales and marketing interactions.

Barriers to Collaboration

Sales and marketing are frequently seen as a single function by other parts of the organization, and customers, a view that contributes to the lack of management of this interface. A CEO said, "Sales and marketing functions have never been separate," but they are distinct disciplines working side by side within the same team (MacDonald 2011, 13). This concept of sales and marketing being the two sides of the same coin more clearly highlight the basic issue between the two groups. They are part of the same department, but with two different, tribal mentalities.

Although a number of barriers to collaboration have been considered, initially three basic categories are considered (Troilo 2012):

1. Cultural (the different beliefs, paradigms, and processes operated within each group)
2. Organizational (conflicting objectives, ambiguous roles, different status of the two groups)
3. Infrastructure (separate physical locations, poor processes, and lack of effective technological infrastructure).

Different backgrounds, philosophies, and management styles within sales and marketing aggravate these barriers. An alternative (but complementary view) is that there are only two sources of friction—economic and cultural. Economically, sales and marketing are "competing" for the same budget (see Diagram 3). Further, different sales and revenue goals are set for each group, which create further economic barriers to collaboration (Kotler, Rackham, and Krishnaswamy 2006). The cultural barrier appears to be, as Lorge (1999), so clearly put it, "Marketers are from Mars, Salespeople are from Venus." While this title is adapted from John Gray's book on the relationship between men and women, it fits rather well as many of the characteristics of marketers and salespeople could be positioned as different as those between "male" or "female." A result of this difference in perception or cultural difference between sales and marketing may lead to a fifth barrier to collaboration and informational conflicts.

The cultural differences between sales and marketing are very real and are based on the development of two different "thought worlds" driven by separate training, competing orientations, and competences. However, it is argued that these different cultures are necessary to perform their functions effectively (Homburg and Jensen 2007). Salespeople are required

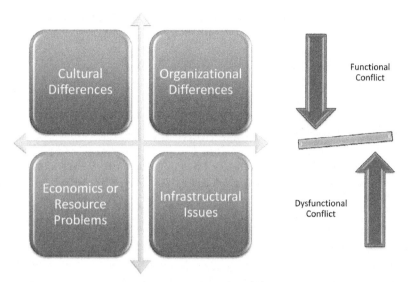

Diagram 3 Barriers to Sales and Marketing Collaboration

to possess solid field experience, strong operational and organizational abilities, and good relational competences. Marketing people should have good analytical skills, the ability to spot trends and undertake creative, strategic thinking. These requirements for the operation of each role frequently lead to the development of a strong in-group identity. Due to these different perspectives, sales believes that marketing is too far away from the customer to understand them properly, while marketing feels that salespeople are too short term and money oriented. These reciprocal stereotypes lead to strengthening barriers. Each side can develop language that is not clearly comprehensible to the other side, and which does not lead to a cohesive organizational identify. The development of these strong in-group identities may also lead to dysfunctional conflict behaviors where information is not shared, objectives are unaligned, and the two groups just rub along rather than collaborate.

The physical separation of salespeople from the rest of the organization may amplify conflict. This separation was illustrated by an organization we visited one Christmas. When asked whether the salespeople would be joining the office party we were told, "*Oh, they do not want to come into the office after all their travelling, so we send them a festive hamper and a card with our best wishes.*" This action did not promote interaction, inclusivity, or collaboration and reinforced the "them and us" culture. As a result, their functional sales identify was more important than the organizational identify. Generally cultural conflicts go deeper than economic ones (Sloane 2010).

Case Study 2

The Barriers Operating between Sales and Marketing

In an organization that we were working with we observed a rather singular set of practices that illustrate how silo working and tension between the sales and marketing functions can affect an organization's market position. The sales and marketing directors within this organization admitted that they have not had a constructive discussion about sales and marketing activities for over five years. The basis for the conflict appeared to be historical. In the past the Sales Director had responsibility and control of the marketing function. There was a strong belief that the sales function did a better job of marketing than was currently happening and there is still some resentment that marketing is no longer in their control. There were comments like "marketing was better when it was run by the sales operations" and "it would help if marketing understood what was happening in the real market place". However, when this historical resentment was unpacked it was discovered that sales had not had responsibility for marketing for more than 10 years and the focus of the organization had changed.

However, there was some justification of the complaints from the sales department. The marketing function in this organization was heavily involved in exchanges with the end user, and did not have any contact with the organizations' customers, who were retailers. Consequently, there was little support for the sales function from marketing, and their brand position was being built through marketing to specialist groups and market influencers. Consequently, sales felt ignored and under resourced even though they were responsible for the survival of the organization, which was sales driven. The rivalry between the directors were causing the sales and marketing departments were acting defensively and to protect their 'territory'. Even the fact that the senior members of staff changed on a fairly regular basis did not change the cultural of distrust between sales and marketing that was embedded in this organization.

Organizational Barriers

The development of organizational barriers to collaboration is present in all organizations, even in smaller organizations. There is a tendency for sales objectives to aim to achieve results in the shorter term, for example: sell on overstocks, meet the next quarter's budget, and achieve particular revenue targets. Whereas marketing objectives tend to be connected to longer-term results such as market share, brand awareness, and market creation. These two different time orientations may work against each other and can remove the awareness of need to work together to align decision and tasks.

The second organizational barrier to collaboration is uncertainty of role and how the departmental roles interconnect. There is a certain amount of crossover in responsibility between sales and marketing roles in that they are both customer facing and have the ultimate objective of attracting customer orders (Cespedes 1995). There is also a tendency for an informal exchange of tasks within the sales and marketing domain. For example, salespeople may evaluate marketing opportunities and design their own promotions, and marketing people may carry out a dialogue with customers, both of which can cause ambiguity in role. This inter-dependency of activities can be a problem without integration mechanisms such as joint planning or informed dialogue. Additional friction may be caused by each function "going their own way," or stepping on each other's toes.

A further source of friction between sales and marketing may occur where there is an expectation by one party (either marketing or sales) to undertake to perform certain activities that either fail to be completed or are not done to expected standards or within the anticipated time slot. Alignment of activities is one of the main challenges facing sales and marketing functions in today's market (Sloane 2010) and it requires a consistent effort from senior managers and both groups to achieve.

Finally on the organizational side, there may be a difference in the status between sales and marketing within the organization that have implications for allocation of resources and decision-making power. An imbalance can lead to a power struggle or a feeling of one party being disenfranchised, and this may be compounded by differences in remuneration. Differences in status can also result in political posturing, with sales feeling that they are unfairly held responsible for success or failure, and marketing feeling ignored for their efforts to achieve success. The result may be opposition, mutual distrust, and dysfunctional conflict. Each of these organizational barriers needs to be addressed if the sales and marketing interface is to operate effectively.

Location Barriers

The location barriers to sales and marketing collaboration are perhaps more visible than cultural or organizational differences and they may be easier to address. In many organizations, sales and marketing are placed in physically separated locations. Sales are located externally to the organization, which gives the impression of a certain self-determining freedom that may cause envy from marketing people that are confined to the office. Further, this physical gap can prevent face-to-face exchanges and the development of social bonds. Technological infrastructures can be designed to help overcome physical barriers, but a lack of proper information systems between the two departments is common (Le Meunier-FitzHugh and Piercy 2006). The lack of an effective technological link can have a negative impact on sharing information and market data. If each group only reviews their own information before making market-related decision, mistakes can be made and misalignments of activities occur, and mutual understanding of shared objectives are harder to achieve.

Inconsistent Processes

Inconsistent practices or processes between sales and marketing are also creating difficulties. For example, poor insights into customer behavior and requirements, or low conversion rates from lead generation. Many organizations are faced with a problem in that marketing collect and create leads, while sales are meant to convert them to revenue. This requires that sales and marketing to collaborate on the lead generation process. Sales and marketing should sit down together and discuss what high or low quality leads look like, when the customers should be "handed-off" to sales, and what constitutes closure. There may be a lack of understanding or disparity in what a well-qualified lead looks like. Salespeople require marketing to provide qualified leads, marketing collateral, a clear brand concept, and an effective system for sharing market information. They expect marketing to support them in the selling process and to integrate their systems to improve the selling situation. The sales and marketing lead generation can be described as a funnel, where marketing "owns" the top half and sales "owns" the bottom, but if the organization splits the funnel into these two parts there is a risk of reducing the business. There should be no boundaries between these two groups and there needs to be a smooth hand over along the funnel (Sloane 2010).

Marketing expect sales to support their marketing messages, build relationships with customers to keep them committed to the organization, and to close the sales. However, they find that sales may consider customers as belonging to them, leading to secretive behaviors and a poor sharing of customer information. Where customer knowledge from sales is not leveraged in the creation of marketing messages, or during the creation of marketing collateral, there is likely to be low confidence in the quality of these activities. Many of these complaints could be eased if there was a better understanding of the role that sales and marketing play in the lead generation process.

Competing for Resources and Budgets

The allocation of resources may also be a substantial barrier to collaboration. The economic constraint relates to the allocation of budgets assigned to each function. Sales need funding to improve the quality of the sales force, while marketing require the same budget to spend on promotions. This friction may be aggravated where the sales force view expenditure of large sums on promotion as a waste of money that should be spent on expanding the sales force (Kotler, Rackham, and Krishnaswamy 2006). There may also be some competition over the promotions budget, with sales requesting point of sales materials, special deals and offers, which may not fit with marketing plans. The marketing team may also be concerned about developing promotions and products that appeal to broad sectors of the market as a whole. The sales force often complains that these elements lack the features, quality or message that their customers require.

Many marketing and sales operations report to the same senior executive, but they are frequently managed separately. This can result in the "left-hand" not knowing what the "right-hand" is doing. Separate management may mean that sales and marketing have to compete for resources. Turf wars can result, especially where marketing are not held accountable for producing revenue, while sales are measured on little else. So even if sales and marketing are working together when something goes wrong it has been known for marketing to blame sales for poor execution for their detailed and brilliant marketing plans, and in turn sales may blame marketing for producing poor collateral and leads, and generally obstructing them in the execution of their role. These attitudes easily turn into competition and a destructive blame culture.

Informational Constraints

Infrequent communications are potentially problematic, especially where sales and marketing remain independently in control of their own specialized knowledge. Marketing people require sales to provide market information (customer and competitor) and use or evaluate the marketing collateral provided. However, there can be difficulties in collating information generated through the sales function, and there may not be processes for market information to be disseminated back to the sales department. Without this feedback sales are not able to evaluate what type of information is useful and understand the benefits of contributing to the informational process (Le Meunier-FitzHugh and Piercy 2006). However, the key complaint from marketing is that sales expect customized marketing collateral for their customers, but they do not provide market information to enable it to be produced. Many of these complaints would be eased with a better dialogue between the two groups. Poor communications can result in confused or stranded customer, incomplete handoffs, and turf wars.

It would be incorrect to believe that small organizations are exempt from these problems (unless the sales and marketing function is performed by the same person). Communication gaps exist in small organizations created by lack of time to brief their colleagues, different targets, and physical separation. Sales and marketing conflict is created by internal competition, but this competition is often more of a mental attitude driven by different objectives.

Outcomes of Conflict between Sales and Marketing

So what are the outcomes of conflict between sales and marketing? Well, they may not be very apparent, as it is unusual for difficulties to be aired in public. The two functions may superficially work well together and the sales and marketing managers may meet regularly to discuss progress, but there may also be a withdrawal from the relationship rather than an increase in collaboration. Further, a lack of collaboration between sales and marketing may result in customers observing inconsistencies in their interactions with the organization, resulting in damage to customer value and relationships. There can also be other problems created. Dysfunctional conflict can lead to a lack of trust that is detrimental to efficient performance (Dawes and Massey 2005). A consequence of dysfunctional conflict may be that sales and marketing stop communicating, resulting in valuable resources being locked into dormant leads that cannot be accessed while the sales and marketing funnel is not operating effectively.

Some of the issues created by dysfunctional conflict are more practical. Sales frequently repurpose documents and materials from marketing, duplicating effort and becoming resentful that they need to do this in their own time. Some research indicates that 80 percent of all marketing generated collateral is not used by salespeople (Aberdeen Group 2002). If sales and marketing are collaborating, marketing can ask sales for feedback on the usefulness of sales collateral. Additionally, marketing collateral can be linked to sales training and core documents may be put online for easy access. Sales can then provide feedback on which tools are really used between the two departments and the content can be built to create a coherent "story" for the customer. Marketing are then able to produce key content and retell the story in a number of different ways.

Once communication between sales and marketing is established sales can provide feedback on the effectiveness of other marketing outputs, for example, adverts and PR. Marketing should acknowledge this input and let sales know what is in the marketing plans for the future.

Summary

In this chapter we have considered how dysfunctional conflict has been created between sales and marketing, and reviewed some of the barriers that have contributed to this conflict. The main barriers have been identified as organizational, cultural, economic, structural, and informational. We have considered how these barriers affect the ability for organizations to generate effective marketing collateral and create/convert new sales leads. Managing the sales funnel may not appear to be an issue to many organizations, but if you consider the cost invested in lead generation, any lead that is lost through lack of coordinated action is effectively a reduction in revenue generation. Organizations have to consider the following when looking at sales and marketing interaction:

- Some conflict will always exist between sales and marketing. The role of the manager is to ensure that this is focused to achieving overall goals.
- Managers should identify which barriers exist in their particular context and then put strategies in place to overcome them.
- Resource allocation is always a contentious issue. Managers need to ensure that resources are allocated in a way that both sales and marketing are able to achieve their objectives. The best option is to have transparency in allocation processes.

In the next chapter we will consider how organizations may overcome organizational barriers.

Key Points

1. Without management attention barriers can form between sales and marketing functions.
2. The barriers may come from a number of sources for example, organizational, cultural differences, economics (e.g., resource issues), infrastructural (including location), and informational.
3. These barriers may add to functional and dysfunctional conflict between sales and marketing.
4. Conflict has the potential to adversely affect lead generation, the development of effective marketing collateral, and customer value.

CHAPTER 3

Alignment and Effective Working Relationships in Lead Generation

Introduction

In the previous chapter we identified a number of barriers to sales and marketing collaboration. One of the most pressing issues with the sales and marketing interface is that of organizational barriers. In this chapter we consider some of the issues and benefits of aligning sales and marketing processes to reduce organizational barriers.

Aligning Sales and Marketing

There is considerable evidence to indicate that there are organizational as well as financial benefits to facilitating an aligned sales and marketing interface. Some studies have found as much as a 47 percent increase in revenues when sales and marketing activities are aligned (Aberdeen Group 2002), but to achieve this a consistent commitment is required, not only from senior managers, but also from sales and marketing personnel. An additional complication is that the market is changing, and sales and marketing roles are changing along with the market. As a result only 32 percent of business believe that their sales and marketing are aligned (Sloane 2010). The question is how should marketing and sales personnel engage with customers? In the past marketers were used to educating customers about the availability and use of new products and services. Now their role is not as clear. Brand management is becoming the main focus in many businesses, and is superseding the more traditional marketing activities of such as providing product information and lead generation.

Sales are also faced with new challenges. Sales personnel are required to interact with customers to unlock value for both parties (Vargo and Lusch 2004). To achieve this it is necessary for personnel to understand how the customer views value, and this pushes sales into responding to their individual customers' needs. An extensive study in Europe has considered five key measures of intradepartmental interaction (information sharing, structural linkages, power, orientation, and knowledge) and identified that there are five different configurations of the sales and marketing within organizations, depending on whether sales or marketing are dominant or cooperative (Homburg, Jensen, and Krohmer 2008). The study (Homburg, Jensen, and Krohmer 2008) has identified that these configurations are Ivory Tower (separate, silo departments with independent knowledge), Brand-Focused Professionals (market-led customer-focused, and mostly consumer goods organizations), Sales Rules (dominated by product expert

Diagram 4 Sales and Marketing Configurations

Source: Homburg, Jensen and Krohmer 2008.

employees with good market knowledge), Marketing-Driven Devil's Advocacy (dominated by a combative, market-knowledgeable department), and Sales-Driven Symbiosis (where there are highly knowledgeable departments with good structural linkages) (see Diagram 4). These differences in power, knowledge, linkages, orientation, and information sharing between sales and marketing underscore the fundamental challenges of aligning their activities. It should be noted however, that the most successful configurations in the European study were Brand-Focused Professionals and Sales-Driven Symbiosis. This indicates that sales success is driven by high market knowledge (whether the most power is held by sales or marketing), and effective processes for sharing knowledge.

Process Alignment

Part of the solution is creating effective processes for sharing knowledge is the creation of dialogue between sales and marketing functions so that they can agree goals, identify crossover areas, and flesh out roles. Apart from agreeing goals and the boundaries of activities, it is important to clarify the parameters within which each group should operate. This process of agreement will also require some flexibility, understanding, and even forgiveness, between the two parties. Senior managers or collaboration facilitators can lubricate this process by acting as a conciliator, or arbiter, when required (Dewsnap and Jobber 2009). Part of the alignment process should also be about agreeing areas of accountability, and consequences of performance. The whole aim of this process is to gain an understanding of each other's point of view, as well as seeking to establish clear working practices and measures of success. These ideas link to the concepts of market knowledge and information sharing that will be explored in Chapter 5.

A technique that may assist with the alignment process is to focus on the concepts of the buyer's persona and the buyer journey. If these can be discussed and agreed then the clashes between sales and marketing activities should be reduced. The sales map can also be agreed with marketing and it should focus on identifying the key data to be shared. Sales and marketing alignment should be a closed loop process with 360-degree view. Overall goals should be aligned, but even if this is achieved sometimes the two groups still have different agendas caused by timescale differences. However, if the practices, targets, and resources can be agreed, then it is possible to manage the different time horizons. The hottest issues for sales and marketing alignment are decreasing values, increasing length of sales cycles, and how to provide feedback on successful leads. This brings us into the area where there has probably been the greatest misalignment between sales and marketing, which is the sticky issue of lead generation and the sales funnel.

Case Study 3
Alignment of Activities

Alignment can take many different forms. One organization that we worked with had been focused on improving the alignment between functional groups for a number of years. When they turned their attention to the sales and marketing functions their first action was to place sales and marketing within the same building. This was based on the belief that they were basically the same function and interacting more frequently. Unfortunately, the sales office and marketing office were initially placed on separate floors, so this action did not achieve the integration that was planned. Upon reviewing the activities of sales and marketing the second plan was to place the two groups in close physical proximity in a new building. The thinking was:- new office, new building, a new start. They were hoping for the benefits of coffee break chats, social interaction and friendships developing between sales and marketing staff would impact on their working alignment. To a certain extent they were successful as informal interactions occurred and there did not appear to be any conflicts in working practices between the two groups. However, the alignment of activities that they were hoping for did not manifest themselves.

The next initiative was to appoint a senior manager to take an overview of sales and marketing activities. While this had some benefits in terms of a common overall objective and joint meetings, it did also result in sales and marketing competing for resources. Further the two functions continued to operate independently to meet their individual targets. On further evaluation we discovered that, although the organization had been undertaking structural adjustments to promote alignment, they had not promoted joint planning, adjusted rewards, or refocused marketing to support sales. Because of some of these issues the old rivalry between sales and marketing continued. Sales did not feel part of the marketing team, and believing that marketing did not support their initiatives. Marketing appeared to be nervous about consulting with sales. Sales was not fully engaged with market research, new product launches or long term strategy because they felt that these activities were not relevant to sales operations. Further, sales appeared to be dissatisfied with marketing activities because there was no clear handover of qualified leads. Marketing even expressed their view of the relationship by saying, "what are sales complaining about, we work well together. We prepare the market for them, find new customers and spend a considerable amount of money promoting the products. All they have to do is collect the orders". Some of these issues were eventually resolved through including sales in strategic marketing meetings, undertaking joint planning for new product launches, engaging in joint sales forecasting and major promotional campaigns, and creating an integrated market research process that included marketing staff meeting with key customers. When these initiatives were implemented the result was an understanding of how the two functions could be mutually supportive.

Lead Generation and the Sales Funnel

Managing the sales pipeline, or sales funnel is one of the principal activities of sales and marketing. The aim is to create, locate, and convert customers to the organization's offer. Traditionally marketing has been at the "front-end" of this process, in the creation and location elements, while sales has been responsible for the "back-end", where the customers are engaged and purchase the offer. However, there are several issues with this apparently simple process, for example, what is a lead? When should the potential customer be "handed" to sales? How many potential leads should be converted? When is a lead dead? Who should be rewarded for achieving the sale and how?

Marketing identifies leads from a number of sources ranging from initial contacts from promotions, through the website, and from agencies. A simple contact address without additional information is an unqualified lead, which creates a great deal of work for the sales person. Sales do not have a clear idea of the lead's requirements and there is a high probability that there will be no sale in the immediate future. This creates a problem with sales forecasting for the sales team. Generally, problems with sales forecasting are caused by a disconnected process and lack of accountability. Therefore, sales forecasting can be improved through cross-functional buy-in and joint planning. Part of cross-functional buy-in is to agree between the sales and marketing teams exactly what a qualified lead constitutes. While this may differ from industry to industry, but there is a general consensus that the qualified lead is one with sufficient substance so that the sales person can engage the prospect correctly. In some cases this will consist of several contacts or "touch points" with the organization while their needs are assessed, before the lead is handed over to sales. These touch points may even consist of the initial direct contact being made by marketing.

Sales need to understand what marketing are doing. While the measurement of contacts (touches) with new customers is important, sales also have to develop existing customers as well as new ones. It is the final resulting sale that is the true measure of effectiveness. The combination of e-links and touches should lead into the sales funnel. It has been suggested that customers receive approximately 10 touches before they purchase. Best practice indicates that information on leads should be clearly defined and consistent within an area, although they may differ across territories. This requires work and communication between sales and marketing personnel. The aim should be to establish wide agreement on the processes within the sales and marketing pipeline. This should be in sufficient detail to allow clear metrics to be applied and for documentation to follow each step. The lead handover process in particular should be broken down so everyone is clear what happens when, and marketing should be able to qualify the lead, before handed over to sales (see Diagram 5). Training should be available so that everyone is using the same terminology in the same way, to prevent misunderstandings.

When designing the sales and marketing sales funnel there are a number of metrics that may be of assistance. One of these is to identify "Lead to Close" time for the organization compared to industry norms. Another calculation would be the number of acceptances compared to the number

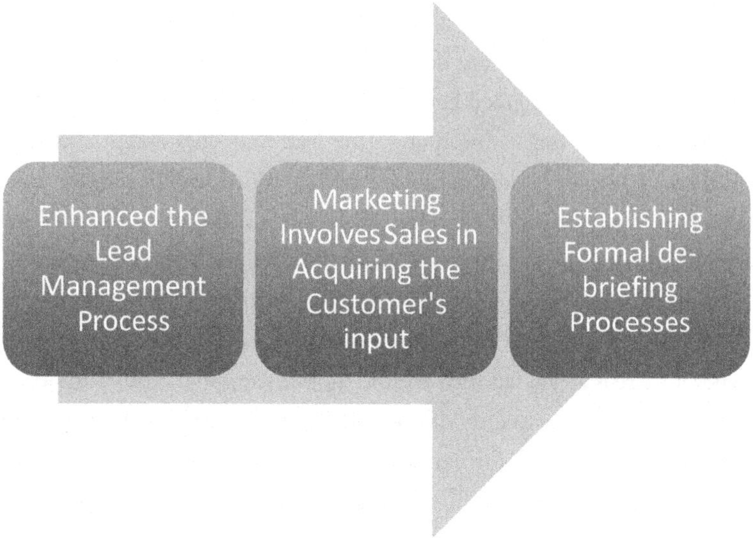

Enhanced the Lead Management Process	Marketing Involves Sales in Acquiring the Customer's input	Establishing Formal de-briefing Processes

Diagram 5 Steps to Success in head generation

of qualified leads generated, to identify the wastage rate. Research has found that 38 percent more sales are closed in organizations where sales and marketing are working in harmony compared to those that do not focus on sales marketing alignment (Sloane 2010). It is also necessary to measure the number of leads progressing at each stage of the process to identify what needs to change to be able to retain the maximum number of leads. This evaluation is important to ensure that progress is measurable and the right rewards can be allocated.

The next challenge in managing the sales pipeline or funnel is data management. Usually this is the responsibility of marketing, perhaps with IT support. Leads should be identified electronically and then pushed through the process. A process flow chart should be produced to allow management to drill down into the detail. Many organizations have this sort of data management system, but if the process is not reviewed and evaluated it is possible to encounter blockages that may lead to a sleeping pipeline. A sleeping pipeline is where leads pile up and tie up resources. The danger is that leads will become old and out of date. To keep the pipeline moving requires effective technical support and platforms. Management should have clear controls and insights into the sales and marketing processes so that they can identify blockages and assign resources to clear them. Service levels should be agreed between parties and levels of service also discussed and agreed. Expectations, goals, measurement, qualification, acceptance, are the key processes in the sales pipeline that should be shared and agreed between sales and marketing.

Consequently, marketing qualify the lead and sales accept the lead, and there should be a clear definition of a qualified lead in different settings. It is also a good idea to clarify when leads should be dropped, in other words a clear rejection code. Sales should only receive "sales ready" leads and documentation should tie down all parties so that they can follow-through each lead to its full potential. It would be beneficial to all parties if there is an agreed turn around on leads and marketing should receive feedback on the quality of the leads. Consequently, the sales person should be able to add information into the database and set up targeted nurturing programs for specified customers. Purchasing and accounting can contribute information on lead conversion, and agree when a sale is deemed to have taken place. Crossover projects should be run to ensure that no leads are left behind. Customers value a seamless experience through the sales process and a comprehensive introduction to the organization. Lead generation has been changing with the development of marketing automation. The integration of data is the basis of relationship marketing.

Consultative Selling

Consultative sales usually appear earlier in the funnel than traditional sales. Creating positive customer experiences and advocacy (through the web) are much more important to consultative selling, where feedback is vital. There should be more shared activities through the lead generation process and each stage should be considered as being aspects of marketing, sales, or deliverables (delivery of the offer to the customer). It can be observed that the start of the sales process, there is an awareness that the customer's journey begins with discovery. Discovery is mostly the responsibility of marketing, but with some sales input, which triggers the events to start engagement, which becomes their joint responsibility. As we move through the customers' journey, the engagement stage is mostly the responsibility of sales with some input from marketing and a little input from deliverables. The evaluation stage of the funnel is still mostly

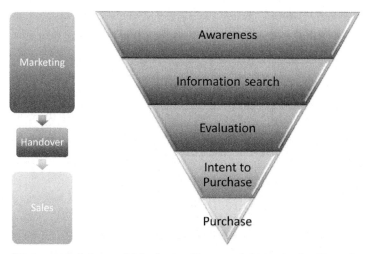

Diagram 6 Sales and Marketing Responsibilities in the Funnel

the responsibility of sales, with some input from deliverables and a little input from marketing. When the customer makes the decision to purchase it is likely to be influenced jointly by sales and deliverables, with very little marketing input. The purchase itself is definitely half sales and half deliverables. The customer experience is defined mostly by the deliverables, with some sales input and a little marketing (fulfillment of expectations). The final stage is mostly the responsibility of deliverables with some input from marketing, in the form of reassurance documentation and the reinforcement of positive messages (see Diagram 6).

Effects of E-Marketing

Web content, such as webinars and case studies can be used to keep prospects engaged, and to provide technical information on the offer, which will probably be produced by marketing. However, sales have to follow up these with relevant contact. Buy-in from sales is critical so that there is a smooth handover between the two groups. Sales is involved earlier than previously through media marketing campaigns and sales cycles. For example, sales can use social media to research potential customers at start of funnel. Marketing automation will help identify leads, but it is measuring messaging effectiveness that will really help to identify where resources should be directed. Consequently, the number of responses to media, the use of advert click rates and identifying the time it takes between the customers searching the web to the sales visit, can all be used to measure effectiveness. Sales and marketing roles in e-marketing are more blurred, but there is a general consensus that marketing should build a website that is linked to the customers' requirements, thereby creating awareness, making initial contact and managing expectations. Their primary aim is still to build brand, but is it critical that marketing should mirror sales messaging.

Selling Direct through the Web

The use of the web as a selling tool is causing some conflict over sales and marketing roles. The first question is who owns the sale? Websites are often built and developed by marketing (as mentioned above), but with the ability to complete the sale through the web it is no longer necessary to hand the customer onto a separate sales department. There needs to be an engagement with this new reality, especially as many organizations have a strategy to direct their small accounts to the web, rather than relying on personal interaction through a sales person. To remove conflict between sales and marketing over this change in role requires an open discussion to identify how these sales are managed and how rewards are allocated. With e-selling growing at an exponential rate in some markets, these discussions are becoming urgent.

How Should Sales and Marketing Work Together?

So the advice for managers, sales, and marketing personnel is to ask the question about how they wish to work together. Gather feedback on what works in your context and establish a dialogue with all parties based on clear metrics. Sales and marketing must be partners and they should have credibility with each other. Sales may own the account, but marketing can provide support and a long-term perspective, which is valuable. Marketing has the broad view, and it is not just about brochures and relationship building. A broad brush is also right for brand management.

It has been argued that, while sales own the customer, it is marketing that owns the funnel. The exception is when the web becomes the marketplace, meaning that marketing can also close and convert leads as well as sales. The trick is to align sales and marketing on the customer's objectives rather than on their internal processes. Consequently, it may be better to think marketing *with* sales rather than sales *and* marketing. Marketing with sales is an integrated process with a feedback loop to the beginning (see Diagram 7). Sales should buy-in on marketing strategy, formation, and implementation. Marketing should be interested in the competitors and new trends exhibited by customers.

The new philosophy is about alignment of sales and marketing processes so that they respond to the buyer's journey in an integrated way (Aberdeen Group 2002). Buyers are much more informed and connected, and they are moving to online conversations rather than face-to-face exchanges. This trend is changing, or blurring, the operation of the sales funnel. Managers should be aware of the hidden sales cycle when forecasting, as well as identifying key points in the marketing with sales process. However, marketing is the front-end of the sales process and they have to make choices about which media to view.

Involvement in planning is the key to success, but try to keep sales and marketing in the right roles and strengthen their involvement. Sales also need the skills or capacity to be able to follow up on the plan. The conversion rate of leads to sales increases when marketing get round the table with sales and understand the sales journey. Programs to help achieve this include opportunity generation and getting salespeople engaged in

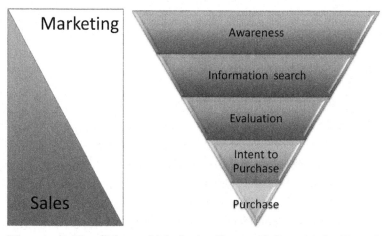

Diagram 7 New Sales and Marketing Responsibilities in the Funnel

setting individual goals. A study of organizations in 84 different countries found that sales and marketing alignment promotes up to a 50 percent growth in sales revenue and 36 percent fewer leads were lost (Macfarlane 2003). It is suggested that marketing could be measured on the usability of leads, while sales are measured on how they use leads, but there should also be metrics to measure the level of sales and marketing collaboration. Accountability is key, but stop sales and marketing fighting over responses and get them to collaborate. Rebuild content for collaboration rather than lead generation.

Summary

This chapter has reviewed the importance of aligning sales and marketing activities. We have also considered how the sales funnel is arguably the greatest area for agreement. Working on aligning processes can allow organizations to streamline their lead generation processes by ensuring that the process is (a) aligned with the organizational strategy and (b) ensures that lead generation are fully qualified before sales resources are allocated, and (c) all parties understand the sales funnel and the value and types of leads that it contains. This should enable that the value of each lead to be identified and the appropriate resources can be utilized so that the full value of the lead is obtained.

Guidance for sales and marketing lead generation:

- Jointly decide who is the ideal customer
- Agree on what a customer looks like (characteristics)
- Define what is a qualified lead
- Agree suitable message content with sales
- Create content that attracts and nurtures prospects
- Focus on customer concerns
- Implement a lead protocol and hand off time line
- Hand off with context and behaviors recorded on line
- Use measurable stats and track to close the loop

The next chapter considers how communication (dialogue) between sales and marketing can be leveraged to improve the alignment between sales and marketing functions.

Key Points

1. Organizational barriers to sales and marketing collaboration may be overcome through alignment of activities and processes.
2. A key area of potential alignment is through the process of new lead generation, the sales funnel.
3. Managing the sales funnel requires sales, marketing, and senior managers to have an open dialogue over roles and how to manage key points in the sales funnel.
4. Aligning activities also requires that sales cooperate with marketing over the development of marketing collateral and engage with marketing planning. Conversely marketing should engage with creating customer value (understanding the customer) and identifying trends in the market place.

CHAPTER 4

How Should Sales and Marketing Communicate?

Introduction

The previous chapter reviewed how sales and marketing activities could be aligned, and recommended that this could be achieved through open and frank dialogue between the parties. This chapter will consider what communication is, and how dialogue can be created and managed for best advantage in the sales and marketing interface.

What Is Communication?

The issues of the type and amount of communications between internal groups have been frequently debated when discussing improving internal relationships. Communication is concerned with the formal and the informal exchanges of information between groups (Anderson and Narus 1990). Obviously, effective communications between groups and across organizational boundaries helps to improve interaction, understanding, alignment and establishing closer interfunctional relationships (Kotler, Rackham, and Krishnaswamy 2006). The argument is that greater communication between sales and marketing functions should enable the development of trust in the abilities of the other party to collaborate (Hughes, Le Bon, and Malshe 2012); Kotler, Rackham, and Krishnaswamy 2006). The problems come from trying to identify how much and what type of communication is optimal in developing this trust and greater understanding.

As communication is such an important part of improving interfunctional relationships it is appropriate to be clear what is meant by communication. Communication has been defined as *"the formal as well as informal sharing of meaningful and timely information."* (Anderson and Narus 1990, 44) There are two main ways of communicating, informal and formal. Informal communications are generated by mutual interest in a topic, while formal communications (e.g., meetings, reports, and e-mails) are usually used for planning, to clarify objectives, allocate activities, and summarize progress. Meeting around the "coffee machine" and exchanging ideas casually, is a good way of keeping communications current (Fisher, Maltz, and Jaworski 1997). However, this informal information exchange may be hard to establish when salespeople are located regionally, and marketing people are generally centrally placed.

The objective in promoting communication between groups is to increase involvement and develop relationships. It is suggested that two significant aspects of cross-functional interaction are the amount and quality of communication and these elements are the ones that are associated with improved relationship commitment (Hulland, Nenkov, and Barclay 2012). The amount of communication is described as the intensity of information flows via e-mails, telephone, formal or informal meetings, and reports (Dawes and Massey 2005). This information flow is relatively easy to measure as it is ordinal, and communication amount may be developed into a metric for looking at levels of collaboration. Studies of communication frequency between functional managers have linked it to greater perceived trustworthiness between players (Becerra and Gupta 2003; Massey and Kyriazis 2007). However, simply increasing the frequency of communication is unlikely to generate maximum benefits for sales and marketing collaboration because information overload can be as detrimental to the relationship as insufficient communication.

The associated concept is communication quality, which may be defined as the extent to which communication between sales and marketing managers is a bidirectional (two-way) process that exchanges credible and relevant information (Dawes and Massey 2005). Of course information is only credible and relevant when it is useful to the receiver. Bidirectional communication can be generated through discussion, and by listening to and responding to each other's feedback on ideas and issues (Dawes and Massey 2005). The aim of bidirectional communication is to be consultative, and to take other's views into account (see Diagram 8). Bidirectional

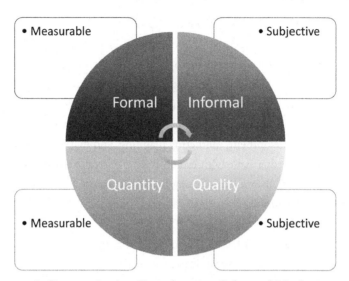

Diagram 8 Communication Types between Sales and Marketing

communication enhances the social aspects of relationships (Massey and Kyriazis 2007). Additionally, exchanging credible and reliable information would help to build trust in the abilities of the other party. Greater trust leads to stronger relationships and an increase in commitment to collaboration (for an additional discussion on trust see Chapter 5). This bidirectional communication can be promoted by formal exchanges facilitated by senior managers, and these exchanges should help to remove the misunderstandings created by isolated thinking and separate objectives (Dawes and Massey 2005; Rouziès et al. 2005). There are a number of areas in which this applies between sales and marketing staff, for example, the generation of market information, joint planning, and lead generation.

There are a number of barriers to interfunctional communications such as how frequently the two groups can exchange information, technical language barriers, and willingness to exchange information (Hulland, Nenkov, and Barclay 2011). The development of specialization in both sales and marketing is one of the main barriers to communication. Each group has developed an individual understanding of information in relation to their own context and perceptions, which develops into their own specialist language. Coded language is usually underpinned by buried or tacit knowledge, whose understanding may create difficulties in translating meanings of particular words or phrases between groups or communities within organization (Oliva 2006). Coded language is frequently created in occupational communities through repeated tasks and actions. However, there is the opportunity to establish communication channels at all levels by reducing the use of coded language, or creating a new joint code that may be built around areas of common ground (Fisher, Maltz, and Jaworski 1997), for example, customer acquisition, new product development, marketing planning, and market information.

There is a further issue with establishing effective communications in that too much communication may be detrimental to collaboration, as a lot of communication, especially formal interaction, can overload the participants (Dawes and Massey 2005). Frequent communications are time consuming, and it has also been found that the quality of exchanges falls as the amount of communication increases (Maltz and Kohli 1996; Fisher, Maltz, and Jaworski 1997). Further, it is suggested that if communication between sales and marketing is forced, the participants may become resentful and the number of misunderstandings tend to increase (Rouziès et al. 2005). Consequently, the recommendation is to focus on effective (bidirectional or consultative) communications that encourages feedback. Further, the development of bidirectional communication that facilitates discussion, information sharing, and shared vision, can lead to higher levels of collaboration between sales and marketing (Dawes and Massey 2005). Establishing the correct frequency and type of communication between groups is an effective way of improving collaboration.

Building Market Information Systems

It is very tempting to ignore the processes involved in collection, storage, and dissemination of market information because they become routines that are not regularly challenged or updated. This occurs even within organizations where current market information is critical to developing responses to rapidly changing market contexts (Fisher, Maltz, and Jaworski 1997). One important element in the development of effective market intelligence is the integration of information from the sales team with information from other sources. Salespeople are in a strong position to provide early insights into the activities of competitors, as well as other changes in the marketplace, so there are good reasons for including the sales team in the design and operation of market intelligence systems. Some problems with collecting information from the sales team are that sales managers are not usually asked to verify the information's accuracy (Evans and Schlacter 1985). Further, in some cases, contributions from the sales teams are kept within the sales department or the sales team does not review the information meaning they are not aware of how it is contributing to the knowledge within the organization.

There is strong evidence to indicate that market information from sales is not being integrated with information from other sources, for example, one study found that only 59 percent of the 204 firms surveyed had any sort of program for capturing market and competitor information through the sales force (Powell and Allgaier 1998). Another issue is that salespeople see their primary role as making sales, and they consequently may not make the effort to be an objective observer or reporter of reliable information. Further, salespeople may be reluctant to pass information on to marketing if there is no clear benefit in doing so (Homburg, Workman, and Jensen 2000). This is especially relevant where their information appears to fall into a "black hole" and they do not receive feedback about its quality and impact.

If the market intelligence system is going to be effective the collection of sales and marketing information should be part of a robust process and the accuracy of the information should be verified. Nonetheless, according to a US survey of 92 managers 46 percent rated sales-generated intelligence as highly important, (Cross et al. 2001) indicating that timely information from the market is valuable. The collection of effective market intelligence gathering is playing an increasingly significant role in informing strategic decision-making as well as marketing planning (Piercy and Lane 2005).

It appears that setting up effective market and competitor intelligence generation processes may be more complex than is generally acknowledged (Aaker 2001). Collecting superior competitive intelligence is so important to business success that some agencies are recommending that there should be a separate unit responsible for managing the resource (Wright, Pickton, and Callow 2002). Establishing a separate unit for market intelligence would ensure that all types of information are included in the analysis and there should be coherent presentation of the results back to all interested parties (Festervand, Grove, and Reidenbach 1988). This should include sales and marketing personnel so that they have common information to base their discussions and decisions upon. One way of ensuring that sales are keen to collect market intelligence is to make sure that the outputs are disseminated back to them. This may seem obvious, but in many cases the market intelligence is available, but the organization's internal processes fail to facilitate prompt and meaningful information exchanges between sales, marketing, and the rest of the organization (Evans and Schlacter 1985).

Case Study 4

Intelligence Systems and Power

There are many horror stories attached to the collection of market information. One organization that we had dealings with (a number of years ago now) was very proud of the reporting systems that they had recently introduced. The objective was the collection of more up-to-date information about customer and competitors activities following each sales representative's visit to the customer. This was before the introduction of IT based reporting systems, so it was a paper-based promotion. There is no issue with this collection method (although paper-based systems can be time consuming). We should say at this point that the organization had thought about the cost in time of filling in reports and had introduced a reward system for sales people. This initiative changed the sales representative's behavior and attitude to data collection and the majority of the data collection forms were completed. Unfortunately, this forward-looking move was not replicated in the office part of the process.

The reports arrived at the office on a weekly basis and the administrative staff then collated them. The reports were carefully filed in date order and the file was then placed on the sales manager's desk. Over the next few days the sales manager read through the reports (depending on his schedule) and he summarized key points. The reports were then re-filed. The information from the data collection was not routinely passed around to management, marketing or even back to the sales representatives. There was no system of dissemination. When we interviewed the sales manager it became apparent that the market information was considered to be a source of power. It was felt that market information belonged to sales. Because the information had to pass though the sales manager's hands it was automatically filtered and only passed on as it was considered appropriate. IT-based technology, of course, should prevent this situation from occurring. Modern market information systems are driven by off-the-shelf CRM systems or sales information systems and the information is available to all interested parties. However, the point of the story is that market information is of little use if it is not disseminated and shared. Information systems rely on managers wanting to engage with the system output. Up-to-date information, especially when it has been validated, can provide detail on new market trends and be a source of competitive advantage.

There could also be a liaison champion in the sales team to help in generating feedback to marketing and thereby helping to improve cross-functional engagement. Marketing should focus on the analytical tools and facilitate engagement by getting sales to buy in. Further, the importance of ensuring that market intelligence does not simply vanish into the organization, so that all parties are motivated to continue collecting and feeding data back to the organization. Marketing have a vested interest in information feedback, but contributions should be acted on or rejected and how it is used should be explained to sales.

Joint Planning

It has been found that joint planning helps to improve collaboration and team working and is a way of generating bidirectional communication. If targets are agreed and set jointly this helps to clarify individual contributions to achieving the overall objectives (Athens 2002). It is suggested that information flows should be tactical as well as strategic, and joint planning would help to clarify the roles of both parties. Both sales and marketing teams should formally meet to discuss how they are going to interact in the future. This may include setting up meetings on areas of common interest as required. In the area of customer acquisition, communication should be continuous across the whole cycle. Processes should be simple, and allow sales and marketing personnel to follow-up with actions.

Planning meetings should not impede processes, but should facilitate them and paperwork should be kept to the minimum, be transparent, and beneficial. Meetings should encourage active listening, so that sales inform marketing about the market, and sales listen to marketing's analysis of market trends.

Communicating with the Customer

There remain a number of significant questions in the sales and marketing arena around the subject of who communicates with the customer, how frequently and in what manner. This question is part of content marketing and includes when and what content to reveal to the customer. With the recent developments in social media, nurturing a potential customer can be automated and Facebook/Twitter/LinkedIn may be used to keep the prospects engaged. These communications are likely to be driven by marketing staff, but there is no reason why sales staff could not be involved in this communication.

There is the move toward putting webinars and workshops on product and service specifications online, as well as a rapid growth in Blogs. These communications have the advantage of being available when the customer requires them and of being interactive. However, these relational roles are infrequently assigned to sales, as marketing often controls the web communications. Consequently, there can be some confusion of role assignment unless managers take steps to clarify communication channels and responsibilities. If marketing is responsible for social media relationships it is even more important for them to work with sales so that the contact with the customer is consistent. Sales and marketing personnel should be communicating the same messages (content and tone). Additionally, social media offers a new way of getting to know your customers. Active listening to blogs, feedback on topics, and general participation in the offer provides a unique opportunity to gain relevant market information.

When the customers are passed onto the sales department they will need details about the communications with that prospective customer so far and on the specific marketing content of these communications. There is also an opportunity for sales personnel to engage with their customers through social media. They can even target the decision making unit (DMU) of their customers through the web, configuring the content for each of the influencers and decision makers. Different companies will have different collateral needs, depending on their situation. Some prospects will need white papers and others will use webinars, some may require demonstrations, and others technical specifications. All online communications should help to identify the type of contact needed by the customer. There should be a coherent dialogue with the prospective and current customers and this is where collaboration between sales and marketing is essential to ensure that this is the case.

A new role that organizations could develop is that of customer advocate, who is central to successful customer communications and appreciates the customer lifecycle process. What can the customer be told that they do not already know? Customers are generally looking for value and expertise so that they can ask informed questions during the exchange process. The salespeople need to understand the organization before they contact the customer. The retention of existing customers and cross selling are two key elements to the successful growth of any business today. There are two perspectives, the customer's and the seller's, and providing a total customer service integrates the views of both these groups. This may be achieved through reviewing customer feedback and putting key elements into the dialogue with the customer and this can only be achieved through sales and marketing collaboration.

New Product Development

Another area where communication between sales and marketing is essential is that of new product development (NPD), particularly in fast moving consumer goods (FMCG) markets, where up-to-date information on new developments and changes in customer and consumer needs are critical to develop new and revised offers. Increasing sales is all about solutions development. Finding solutions for customers' and consumers' current and future needs can only be achieved if information from the sales and marketing interface is integrated (Guenzi and Troilo 2007). Therefore, effective communications between sales and marketing, and then with other parties in the NPD team, will underpin the conceptualization process. Further organizational performance is not just about conceiving and developing the appropriate solutions and products; it is also about how these are implemented. Implementation difficulties have been cited as one of the main reasons for the failure of some innovation projects (Dougherty 2001).

Research has found that there is a positive link between the effectiveness of the sales and marketing relationship, superior customer value and sales (Biemans, Brenčic, and Malshe 2010). The successful implementation of innovation projects are reliant on the sales and marketing personnel being collaborative as possible as they are involved in converting the new product offers into understandable concepts for the customers. The coherent implementation of the innovation needs all parties to exchange information and expertise, and this may be facilitated by collaborative cross-functional relationships (Massey and Kyriazis 2007; Olson, Walker, and Ruekert 1995). Improving the success rate of new product deployment is important for all organizations, as new products have major strategic implications in medium to long-term cash flows, and even in the long-term survival of the organization (Cooper 1996). Successfully implementing new offers is a crucial process for the long-term future of organizations, particularly those competing in cutthroat environments. The role of sales and marketing in this NPD process can only be achieved through consistent communications and the sharing of information, ideas, and concepts in both the development stage and at the implementation stage (launch of the new products).

Summary

Informational constraints revolve around the physical difficulties of sales and marketing communication as well as sharing and disseminating information. Poor communications between sales and marketing may be created through the development of separate identities and coded language. Sales use their own language to discuss customers and their relationship with them. They also think in a different time frame from marketing. Marketing has its own specialist language to describe different marketing campaigns and the information from analytics, which can cause a lack of understanding and frustration between the two groups. Physical location has already been discussed, but it also has the effect of impeding bidirectional communication, especially if it is not supported by a suitable technological infrastructure. Sharing information and taking joint decisions can be negatively affected by poor communications. It has also been identified that sales and marketing play a key role in bringing new innovation projects to the market and it is critical that both parties ensure that they are communicating the same benefits and reasons to purchase to the customer.

- Organizations need to consider the formalization of processes to ensure that communication is sufficient and effective.
- Each party should understand the role that they play in the collection, storage, and dissemination of market intelligence.
- Communications with customers must be consistent wherever it originates from within the organization.

The next chapter will consider how sales and marketing can build relationships with customers.

Key Points

1. Communication can be formal or informal, and may be measured through the amount of communication traffic taking place and through the quality of information being communicated.
2. There are a number of areas that can provide opportunities for sales and marketing to improve the amount and quality of communications between sales and marketing.
   a. Market information
   b. Joint Planning
   c. Innovation, generation, and implementation
3. Market intelligence systems should require the integration of input from both sales and marketing sources, and should be fed back to all parts of the organization.

CHAPTER 5

The Role of Sales and Marketing in Customer Relationships

Introduction

In the previous chapter we considered the role of communication between sales and marketing and how it affects lead generation, market intelligence, and collaboration. This chapter will move into the relationship with the customer and how trust performs an important part in the sales and marketing relationship as well as the relationship with the customer. How customer value can be increased through co-creation will be considered. Co-creation of value is the concept that customer can become partners in the co-production of the offer being made to them.

Customer Focus and Relationship Building

There is a growing emphasis on building customer relationships as increasing competition and demanding customers drives the need for organizations to design more complicated offers for their customers (in terms of the combination of services and physical products). Sales and marketing personnel are at the customer interface and all market-oriented organizations are being driven to adopt a relationship-building approach to marketing and the management of other external networks (Grönroos 1994; Harker and Egan 2006). On the whole, it is impossible for organizations to operate without forming some sort of relationship with their customers (Blois 1998), although these will vary in terms of their nature and length. In some cases a business connection may consist of nothing more than a single exchange, but even in this short interaction a reassurance and a feeling of being "cared for" can be created.

At the other end of the spectrum is an extended relationship in which both customer and seller have a shared interest in creating a mutual long-term commitment (Palmer 1994). This relationship will be created through a number of purchases over an extended period, which may result in the mutual exchange of ideas and services. "Customer relationships are not just there; they have to be earned." (Grönroos 1990, 4) Although the essence of this statement may seem straightforward and obvious, the issue of how positive customer relationships are earned and developed remains under discussion. Customers will frequently select to trade with organizations that are either well established or who have reassured them through marketing commuications of the quality of their offer. From the customers' and consumers' point of view, stable relationships with a seller are particularly important if they perceive high levels of risk in the purchase process (Palmatier et al. 2006). Perceived risk and uncertainty are particularly high for customers when they are contacting new suppliers. Consequently, high value or complex offers will require that the customers trust the seller to deliver on the value promised. The customers who consume services and products over time will both benefit from extended relationships and greater trust (Baumann and Le Meunier-FitzHugh 2014; Crosby, Evans, and Cowles 1990). These extended relationships will deliver tangible and intangible benefits to the participants, for example, there are personal benefits from social interaction such as increased knowledge, friendship and satisfaction, as well as physical (product) or financial benefits (Dwyer, Schurr, and Oh 1987; Sheth and Shah 2003).

Marketing theory and practice has established that it is more expensive to constantly attract new customers than to retain existing ones (Hennig-Thurau, Gwinner, and Gremler 2002; Sheth and Parvatiyar 1995). Consequently, organizations should strive to attract and maintain loyal customers (Berry 1995) and sales and marketing are at the heart of this endeavor. Marketing can establish communications with both potential and existing customers, ensuring that they are informed, reassured, and encouraged to continuing the relationship. Communications may take a number of forms, including social media, advertising, and through customer services. Although salespeople have traditionally had a more direct relationship with the customers, recent developments in technology have meant that marketing have direct interaction with customers. However, on the whole sales are in a stronger position to establish lasting ties through developing an interest in their customers' activities and the co-creation of value. Customers are the arbiter of the value they receive from the offer and they understand the solution that they are seeking (Vargo and Lusch 2004).

The collaboration of sales and marketing functions is essential to developing sustainable relationships between the organization and the customer. To achieve this it is suggested that sales and marketing are integrated into the process of communicating with the customer, so that they are "selling" the same value. Sales and marketing should be encouraged to meet customers and ask distributors and agencies how the product should be brought to market. Additionally, sales should help with the provision of positive testimonials to be used as PR (or case studies) and on the website to reassure customers about the value of the offer. Together sales and marketing people should be able to reassure the customer that their offer has the value required to meet the customer's needs, and thereby establish a lasting relationship with that customer.

Successful buyer and seller relationships are two way, as not only do suppliers have to attract loyal customers, but buyers want to find organizations that elicit their loyalty as well (Berry 1995). A long-term relationship to a supplier significantly promotes feelings of security and confidence, while lowering anxiety (Biggemann and Buttle 2009; Hennig-Thurau, Gwinner, and Gremler 2002). Whoever is generating and sustaining the relationship, however, it has to be highlighted that organizations should determine what kinds of relationships are suitable for individual customers (Harker and Egan 2006; Sheth and Shah 2003). The type of relationship that is the most productive also differs between industrial sectors, although long-term relationships are particularly high in industries that have strong degree of "people focus, customer contact time per interaction, customization and discretion, and process focus" (Guenzi and Georges 2010, 115). The result is that continuing beneficial customer relationships is correlated to business success.

Case Study 5

Benefits of Forming Sales and Marketing Partnerships

We have spoken to many organizations about collaboration between sales and marketing acknowledge, and they have always acknowledged its importance to organizational success. However, these organizations also say that they have excellent sales and marketing relationships within their organization. When we have given talks on the topic the delegates also are inclined to say, 'well we know all of this'. However, over the years we have struggled to find many organizations that have really integrated their sales and marketing activities. Achieving collaborative sales and marketing relationships appears to be a very difficult thing to do.

One organization in the food industry has gone further than most in achieving collaborative sales and marketing relationships. Their customer base was large supermarket chains. A few years ago they realized that the two things that they at which they had to excel at to enable them to start a meaningful dialogue with their buyers were: A) Get their deliveries right. The reason for this was that they found that their sales people were spending a considerable amount of their time discussing delivery issues rather than selling, so that up to half their visit was wasted and they were always on the back foot. B) To ensure that they knew more about the customer's final end user's needs and wants than the supermarket did. This is where sales and marketing collaboration came to the fore. They had put in rigorous and robust systems for collecting and disseminating market intelligence. Sales and marketing were actively encouraged to share this information and analyze it to reveal market insights. They also ensured that the marketing systems were in place to support the sales operation and to achieve this they had put dedicated marketing personal around the various sales teams. As one of their managers said to us "there are no secrets between sales and marketing. It is not acceptable for staff to withhold information or to have ownership of information. It belongs to the company, that is it, belongs to us all". Marketing staff, as part of the selling team, also attended meetings with buyers and there was a degree of fluidity of staff moving around the customer-focus teams. The people in the organization did admit that this structure was not easy to implement and that there were, unfortunately, some casualties. However, everyone supported the change in the long run, as they found that it made them more nimble and flexible in the market place and more successful in terms of sales and profitability.

Trust between Buyers and Sellers

One of the functions of the organization is to create successful relationships with their customers. This can be achieved by establishing trust, commitment, and satisfaction in the relationship (Crosby, Evans, and Cowles 1990). It has been found that customer satisfaction with the organization can translate into trust. Trust in the seller in turn leads to increased commitment on behalf of the buyer to the organization (Ulaga and Eggert 2006). Organizations should be encouraged to maintain customer satisfaction through focusing on the customer's needs, and thereby encouraging the development of trust. Trust is at the center of any human interaction, as it allows relationships to develop. It has been found to exist between both individuals (*interpersonal trust*) and between organizations or brands (*interorganizational trust*) (Guenzi and Georges 2010). However, only individuals can experience trust because it is based on attitudes, beliefs, perceptions, and emotions that only people can experience (Mouzas, Henneberg, and Naudé 2007).

Interpersonal trust is helpful is particularly developing collaboration between sales and marketing functions. There are two types of interpersonal trust: cognition-based and affect-based trust (McAllister 1995; Rousseau et al. 1998).

1. Cognition-based trust is the recognition that the other party is skilled, or expert in some way that is relevant to the relationship, and we are reassured that they will be able to fulfill our expectations. This type of trust is important between the sales and marketing functions. It is helpful to their relationship if one party can rely on the other to perform their part of the operation efficiently and effectively.

2. Affect-based trust is based on emotional bonds that form between the participants in the relationship. This part of trust usually develops over time and can be very effective in establishing a strong and lasting sales and marketing relationships.

These trust bonds are usually based on the belief that the other party will act in the best interests of the relationship (Johnson and Grayson 2005). Cognitive-based trust is the foundation of interpersonal trust as it is based on the competences of both parties, which can lead to affect-based trust, which is the feeling that the relationship is secure, strong, and reliable. Where it is established between individuals, affect-based trust can deliver additional benefits that are not created through cognitive-based trust (McAllister 1995). The development of interpersonal trust means that sales and marketing are likely to be predisposed to collaborate with each other.

Trust can also be helpful in developing relationships between the customer and the organization. Customers may trust the organization's brand or reputation before they begin interacting with it and then develop interpersonal trust with individual sales or marketing personnel. Trust may be initiated and developed at the beginning of the relationship, but a bad experience or failure to meet customer satisfaction can quickly damage the trust that has been built up. It is also argued that trust is unreliable in predicting successful business relationships because the nature of trust changes over time (Mouzas, Henneberg, and Naudé 2007; Ulaga and Eggert 2006).

Three types of interorganizational trust have been identified (contractual trust, competence based trust, and goodwill-based trust) (Sako 2002). These types of interorganizational trust broadly relate to cognitive and affect-based trust of interpersonal trust, with the addition of a belief that the other party will meet their contractual obligations. Interorganizational based trust does not mean that the institutions trust each other, but that the employees of one business have trusting attitudes toward the other business (Mouzas, Henneberg, and Naudé 2007). To create trust in business relationships it is necessary for sales and marketing to demonstrate knowledge, skills, and capabilities in the field so that competence based trust can be established. This type of trust then may or may not lead to the more emotional form of trust (goodwill-based trust) that can create ties that are more difficult to break, and that can create more profitable and longer relationships (McAllister 1995; Zaheer, McEvily, and Perrone 1998). Creating trust in the organization is also helpful in allowing customers to transfer their relationships to new employees when employees change roles. The combination of organizational trust, routines, and

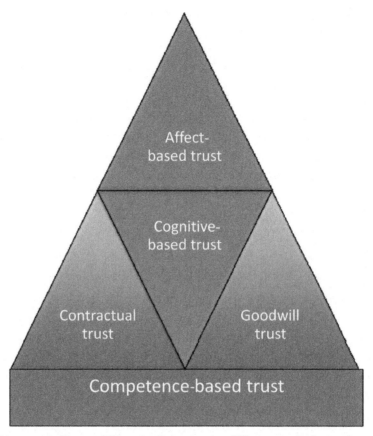

Diagram 9 Types of Trust in Organizational/Customer Relationships

processes allows the mutual commitment that is established between individuals to be extended, adopted, and taken for granted by new members of staff. There are many instances where "organizations" have managed to extend relationships, even when the personnel change, because they have created interorganizational trust (see Diagram 9).

Sales and marketing are central to establishing both interpersonal and interorganizational trust in all its customer relationships. The reciprocal relationship between interpersonal and interorganizational trust is usually located in the routines and practices of both organizations and their personnel (Baumann and Le Meunier-FitzHugh 2014). Sales and marketing collaboration can also affect interorganizational trust by the way that they interact with each other. Sales and marketing functions that are not collaborating may adversely affect the customer's view of the organization, in particular their trust in sales and marketing messages.

There are many stories from practice of how customers have been able to play different people and departments "off against each other" to get better deals. This is especially evident if customers have been mailed offers from the organizations that have originated from marketing, which the salespeople are unaware of or are not able to match. One example of this was an antidotal story we heard were an organization in the food industry suffering from a break in the supply chain. The marketing department took the initiative and wrote to customers informing them of the impending stock shortage and encouraging them to forward order. Unknown to them this was a ploy that sales had been using for years to get customers to forward order during the slow part of the sales cycle. The result was to undermine the credibility of the sales personnel and create a lack of trust in the organization. A coordinated message, and collaboration between sales and marketing would have avoided this situation. Within the customer relationships interpersonal and interorganizational trust are intertwined and both have to be considered when building relationships (Das and Teng 2001; Zaheer, McEvily, and Perrone 1998). Sales and marketing collaboration should provide a sound basis for developing healthy, trusting relationships with customers.

Value Co-Creation

Another element that is important to establishing profitable business relationships is that of value co-creation. Creating value for the customer occurs through the offer that is made by the organization through sales and marketing interaction with the customer (Prahalad and Ramaswamy 2004). Value can comprise of the intangible elements of the offer such as delivery times, warrantees, and brand, as well as physical elements such as color, features, and quality (duration, experience, and quality for service offers) (Woodruff and Flint 2006). Value is therefore something that is experienced at the individual level by the customer and the seller, and has different meanings to each party. The concept of co-creation is rooted in the interaction between two parties. So it is possible for customers to gain greater value from an interaction with one organization than from

Diagram 10 Customer Value Co-Creation

another, because of the specific combination of tangible and intangible benefits offered.

Co-creation of value is located in the boundary-spanning personnel, such as sales and marketing because they are the main point of contact with the customer (see Diagram 10). Consequently, they can engage with the customer's value chain and facilitate value fulfillment, allowing the seller to identify what the customer means by value, and helping the customer to explore what value the seller can provide. The customer is not passive in co-creation of value, as value is jointly realized through their interaction with the organization (Vargo and Lusch 2011). To ensure value co-creation is maximized, sales and marketing have to decide what type of interaction the customers prefer. It is then possible for the organization, through sales and marketing, to utilize their customer and product knowledge to create superior customer experiences, value, and consequently competitive advantage (Grönroos 2011; Payne, Storbacka, and Frow 2008). The relationship between sales and marketing is critical in creating this type of interaction, because unless sales and marketing staff communicate with each other they will not be able to understand their capabilities and the customers needs, so they will not be able to engage in meaningful customer value co-creation.

Summary

Customer relationships are at the heart of successful exchanges and they may be built on individual transactions, or through extended relationships, but they must all create value for the customers. Establishing collaborative sales and marketing operations allows for the creation of greater customer value, based on clear customer knowledge between sales and marketing. It is necessary for sales and marketing to align their activities with the organizational objectives. It should be clear what makes the organization's offer unique, and what exactly is the value proposition that is being made to customers?

Interpersonal trust between sales and marketing can be built on demonstrations of competence leading to cognitive-based trust. As the interaction continues affect-based trust may be created so that sales and marketing become more aligned and collaborative. Competence also underpins the trust between the sales and marketing functions and the customer. If the customer trusts the organization's ability to deliver the required value and believes that their contracts will be honored, the foundation for interorganizational trust in the brand is created, and effective buyer and customer relationships can be established.

The main issue with establishing customer relationships is that the relationship changes over time, sometimes for the better and sometimes for the worse. In reality customer's requirements change, and energy in maintaining the relationship can run out. Consequently, it is up to the organization and their representatives to maintain the relationship and put the effort into revitalizing the offer, and establishing trust. We believe that this can only be achieved effectively with the sales and marketing functions that are collaborating effectively to ensure that all aspects of the relationship with the customer are being identified and realized.

- The value proposition should be collaboratively developed between sales and marketing.
- The value proposition should communicate to the customers through their web and media contacts as well as through direct sales contacts.

- Organizations should embrace their customers, create contractual and competence based trust, use language that the customer understands to build goodwill-based trust to maintain relationships.

The next chapter looks at ways in which managers can facilitate sales and marketing collaboration.

Key Points

1. Building effective relationships with customers is fundamental to identifying customer value and to co-creation of value.
2. It is important not only to build interpersonal trust between sales and marketing to build collaboration, but also to build trust with the customer in the sales and marketing relationship.
3. Customers build trust not only with the individuals within the organization, but also in the organization itself.
4. Sales and marketing need to work together not only to understand customer's needs, but also to create an environment where the value proposition can be communicated.
5. Sales and marketing play a critical role in translating the value proposition so that co-creation of value can occur.

CHAPTER 6

Managing the Sales and Marketing Interface

Introduction

We have seen in the previous chapter how collaboration between sales and marketing functions is critical in building trusting relationships between sales and marketing, and the customer. Sales and marketing also create the environment where the organizations vision and value proposition are communicated to their customers. This chapter will look at the role that senior managers play in building collaborative sales and marketing relationships.

Motivating Collaboration

One of the key questions for senior managers is how to manage cross-functional interactions. As functional groups have become more specialized in their roles the reality of "silo working" has been created in many organizations. "Silo working" is where departments work closely with their colleagues to create specialist groups with their own language, behaviors, and knowledge, which may not necessarily interact with other functional groups (Homburg, Jensen, and Krohmer 2008). To break down silos senior managers should *"consider programs that encourage departments to achieve goals collectively, have mutual understanding, work informally together, ascribe to the same vision and share ideas and resources"* (Kahn 1996, 147).

However, there are a number of barriers to engendering collaboration and as the costs to the organization can be high. To create new learning and innovation requires the input of time, and this can cause interruptions in working patterns, creating stress and cross-functional working has been prone to failure (Willcock 2013). There is the additional problem with the sales and marketing interface in that senior managers can set different targets and goals for the sales and marketing teams. These differences in goals can cause the two groups to pull in different directions and may create friction. Unfortunately, it is very difficult for managers to ignore the urgent need to meet sales targets, even when the strategic goals of the organization may require a different strategy.

Managers should be aware of the need to create collaborative environments and align goals and activities so that the short-term targets are met without compromising the longer-term objectives. Research has indicated that business growth can be around 5 percent faster in organizations where processes are aligned (Sloane 2010). This is unlikely to happen by itself and senior managers should focus on removing barriers and identifying areas of potential friction (Piercy 2006). Sales and marketing personnel may respond in a defensive way to integrate their behaviors and this could lead to reinforced attitudes toward the other group (Willcock 2013). A solution is to clarify roles, noting areas where there is mutual dependency and where there may be role ambiguity. The use of joint planning and shared objectives, while still retaining the independent views of sales and marketing (Cordery 2002; Schmonsees 2006) appears to be the key to success. If targets are set jointly then individual contributions to achieving overall objectives can become explicit, thereby encouraging better working practices. Further, mutual understanding of each other's roles can be achieved through undertaking of cross-functional activities.

Marketing literature has suggested that there are a number of integration mechanisms that may be employed to reduce tension and improve sales and marketing relations (Dewsnap and Jobber 2000; Kotler, Rackham, and Krishnaswamy 2006). These integration mechanisms can range from formal to informal or from structural to managerial initiatives. Various structural mechanisms for example, project teams, task forces, or steering committees have been suggested to improve interdepartmental relationships. Additionally, tools such as personal meetings, e-mails and teleconferencing, and human resource systems including job rotation, joint planning, and equal reward systems (Child 1985; Leenders, Janszen, and Wierenga 1994) are also thought to be beneficial. Differences in culture and perspective, and a lack of understanding of how each other's roles are linked may be improved through some of these cross-functional mechanisms. On a more practical note it should be possible through cross-functional working for sales and marketing to be able to demonstrate products and service features and to understand the uniqueness of the offer.

Integration Mechanisms

Integration mechanisms allow for the exchange of interdepartmental information and the creations of joint activities, for example, planning sessions, team working, and meetings. It has been suggested that operating performance is related to human performance, that is, personal capability, individual motivation, and the ability to work together (Homburg, Jensen, and Krohmer 2008; Shapiro 2002). Consequently, by improving people's ability to work together it is possible to improve operating performance. If marketing conceptualizes campaigns, manages the market knowledge, and provide sales support, while sales staff manage customer relationships, provide market and product information and act as the customer advocate, then it is important to make sure that the two groups have the ability to interact positively.

There have been a number of suggestions for effective integration mechanisms between sales and marketing, including cross-functional meetings, training sessions, job rotation, and cross-functional projects (Le Meunier-FitzHugh and Piercy 2007; Rouzies, et al. 2005). The aim of these activities is to provide interaction opportunities as well as provide experiences of successful collaborations. Being involved in cross-functional meetings is probably the most effective mechanism, as these meetings can include sharing market information, forward planning, alignment of goals as well as an opportunity to get to know each other's priorities and characters. Job rotation, cross-functional training, cross-functional teams, provides an ideal opportunities for interaction, and these are usually managerial initiatives (see Diagram 11).

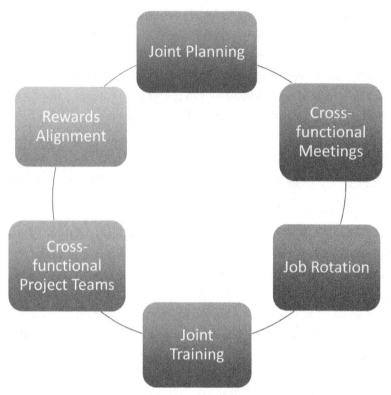

Diagram 11 Managing Sales and Marketing Integration

Cross-Functional Meetings and Joint Planning

Joint meetings to aid planning and the setting of integrated targets and objectives, are recommended. Senior managers can set up formal meetings to assist with information sharing that are essential to promote shared understanding and also to enable the participants to act on the same information rather than their own perspectives (Juttner, Christopher, and Godsell 2007). Joint meetings may also help to establish discussions on concepts and practices, so that they can be clarified to prevent misunderstandings (Oliva 2006). Regular meetings can also help to break down silo thinking and provide opportunities to review progress, identify openings in the market, and build collaboration (Kotler, Rackham, and Krishnaswamy 2006). However, there is a danger that too many meetings may overburden participants and can lead to an overload of information (Kahn 1996). One suggestion is that cross-functional meetings should occur once a month and that sales and marketing teams should spend up to 30 percent of their time on cross-functional matters to improve collaboration between departments (Armstrong et al. 1996). Another suggestion is that formal meetings are more successful if supported by informal interactions over the coffee machine, through the intranet, or telephone, so that ideas can be freely developed and information swiftly exchanged (Rouzies et al. 2005).

The key to successful meetings is to gain agreement on future direction and processes. There should be a strategy that can be rolled out by marketing or sales personnel, and this should be developed through joint planning. The aim would be for the marketing and sales managers to reach agreement on the strategies adopted for each product and service (Dewsnap and Jobber 2000). Processes should also be aligned so that there is one journey for the customers, from promotion through leads to close. The customer's experience is the essential element. Both sales and marketing personnel should be able to engage with the customer to identify the value the customer requires. The customer's journey is facilitated by appropriate marketing collateral that enhances the customer experience and moves them toward purchase (Le Meunier-FitzHugh et al. 2009). This integration of message and alignment of activities cannot be created without joint formal planning. So integrate sales and marketing on the development and delivery of customer value.

Cross-Functional Teams

A critical role of senior management is to facilitate the creation of cross-functional teams through the provision of the right structures, definitions of roles and clear leadership (George, Freeling, and Court 1994). To encourage the collaboration cross-functional teams can be created to either complete specified processes (e.g., lead creation or handling market information), or to undertake projects. Cross-functional teams have been found to bridge communication gaps between internal groups (Shultz 1998). Importantly, cross-functional teams foster the ability to become more effective in decision making, and to share and act on market information developed through cross-functional working (Cohen 1993). Further, a significant increase in output has been noted from cross-functional teams over that from autonomous, functional groups (Juttner, Christopher, and Godsell 2007; Krohmer, Homburg, and Workman 2002). These improvements in output may arise from a combination of a clearer understanding of any possible issues, increased familiarization with each other's objectives and a sense of ownership of decisions (Juttner, Christopher, and Godsell 2007; Krohmer, Homburg, and Workman 2002). Another key benefit is that employing cross-functional teams can establish behaviors and processes that are conducive to collaboration (Leenders, Janszen, and Wierenga 1994; Mohrman 1993). In other words during the project and team work links are established between key individuals that may be maintained after the conclusion of the project. Cross-functional teams also allow for the development of joint initiatives and market planning (Dewsnap and Jobber 2009).

In addition to cross-functional teams sharing common objectives, joint working helps personnel to share achievements, as well as experiences and perspectives. It should be noted that the use of cross-functional teams is not required for the formation of formal or informal integrating roles, for example, liaison positions or coordinating roles, but some recent research has indicated that some formal integrating roles like trade marketing or category management positively influenced the level of collaboration between sales and marketing (Dewsnap and Jobber 2009). Another suggestion is for the creation of open teams to help the group be flexible and responsive to change (Willcock 2013). An open team has links outside the project that provide new information and feedback, improving the team's ability to review how things are working through interaction with other sales and marketing personnel. Although employing cross-functional teams could indicate that sales and marketing are one function, it should be noted that specialists roles continue to be necessary for the successful operation of the department, and consequently retaining the different perspectives and skills has been found to be essential to effective operations (Homburg and Jensen 2007).

Cross-Functional Training

Where sales and marketing departments are experiencing role ambiguity, there may be a lack of understanding of each other's roles and of the other party's needs (Bals, Hartmann, and Ritter 2009). It is suggested that one way to address this lack of understanding is through cross-functional training (Kahn 1996; Matthyssens and Johnston 2006). Cross-functional training may take the form of sales and marketing working on either sales or marketing skills, or on problem solving skills. Training is not only about the benefits of improving skills sets for example, learning about sales techniques or about marketing skills, it is about allowing groups to interact and, through joint problem solving, learn about each other's strengths. It is through education that participants will be able to align their activities and make formal (informal) connections between roles. Cross-functional training will also assist with joint problem solving of common issues and develop personal links with co-workers (Cohen 1993; Lawrence and Lorsch 1975).

There are problems with cross-functional training however. Training allows people to act "out of role," and to be vulnerable to evaluation. It has been highlighted that some members of staff may be uncomfortable performing "out of role"' as they may worry about lack of proficiency or making mistakes that would make them look foolish (Moenaert and Souder 1990). There can also be natural tensions between different personalities (Willcock 2013), and sales and marketing people have a tendency to have very different personalities and perceptions. In addition, there is an opportunity cost of taking personnel away from their specialist roles. Consequently, there is a disincentive to take part in cross-functional training as it could result in reduced employee productivity in the short term. It has also been identified that where there is forced interaction between groups the resulting relationship was found to be less than optimal. However, to bridge the gap between sales and marketing, cross-functional training may be used to help develop an understanding of each other's perspectives and skills, and thereby opening the way to higher levels of collaboration (Guenzi and Troilo 2006; Homburg and Jensen 2007). Further, it is possible to reduce conflict between internal groups through a variant of training programs, especially when supported by other integration mechanisms and focusing on meeting the needs of the customer.

Job Rotation

If integration mechanisms are managerial initiatives intended to promote interaction and collaborative behavior within organizations, then one of the most powerful tools should be job rotation. Job rotation is where personnel are allowed to "walk in the shoes" of their counterparts. Job rotation builds mutual understanding and therefore promotes an environment where collaboration can be established (Rouzies et al. 2005). Job rotation may also open lines of communication between sales and marketing staff by providing the participants with a common background or frame of reference so that they have an understanding of how their work contributes to achieving overall goals.

The aim would be for marketing staff to join salespeople on calls and establish relationships with customers. This may take the form of working as a sales person for a short time. Some organizations have realized the benefit of this action and require their marketing staff to work as salespeople before going into the marketing office. The reciprocal arrangement would be for sales staff to partner marketing people during a specific task for example, launching a new offer, carrying out market research or designing a promotion. However, this practice is relatively uncommon, and is something that could be usefully developed. If sales personnel are given the opportunity to work in the marketing office at the beginning of their career they become aware of the challenges and opportunities facing the marketing role. The use of job rotation should allow members of one specialism to experience the tasks that the other group performs. Job rotation also highlights differences in culture, working practices, and objectives, and helps to demystify roles and language. Job rotation between sales and marketing may also be instrumental in helping to transfer market information and good practice (Dewsnap and Jobber 2000; Rouzies et al. 2005; Krohmer, Homburg, and Workman 2002).

Sales and marketing staff should be encouraged to understand each other's work and to understand the roles that they both play in achieving objectives. It is also possible to enable sales personnel to contribute to marketing planning, and tactical level marketing, while marketers could experience the sales process (Kotler, Rackham, and Krishnaswamy 2006). The biggest weakness of job rotation is that the transferred members of staff may have few skills relevant to the new job area, and consequently may feel out of place and learn little from the experience. Further, poor performance by exchanged members of staff may reinforce negative serotypes. However, on the whole job rotation has been found to be beneficial in overcoming uncertainty and mistrust between sales and marketing, and to help in establishing more positive working relationships (Juttner, Christopher, and Godsell 2007; Matthyssens and Johnston 2006).

Case Study 6
Effects of Sales and Marketing Reward Structures

There have been many debates about the importance of aligning rewards between sales and marketing. However, the more that we engaged with the debate, the more we have come to realize that it is very complex topic and that there is no single fix. From our research into sales and marketing rewards we have found that standard way of rewarding sales personal is through a basic salary with commission. The standard way of rewarding marketing is with a more substantial salary, with maybe a bonus based on organizational success. The disadvantage of this system is that there is little linkage between the activities on which they are being rewarded. Further, there is always a danger of rewarding the wrong sort of behaviors. Sales people can aim to manage their territories to gain the maximum commission, and there is little ownership from marketing people of sales outcomes. A number of organizations have experimented with different systems to try to improve this situation, but they have found it to be challenging. There is usually a resistance to change from staff and frequently there is a misunderstanding of why the change is taking place.

One organization that chose to change their reward structure started by reviewing their sales force activities and they found that there was a tendency for the reward structure to reward behaviors that were not always beneficial to the organization, e.g. holding back orders to meet future targets or pushing for orders before the customer was really prepared to buy. They also wanted the sales force to change the way that they interacted with the customers and move towards a more long-term relationship, rather than continuing with a more transactional relationship. They wanted to remove the need to gain immediate sales and allow for more customer focus and development, but they recognized that there were inherent dangers in doing this. A second objective was to align sales and marketing relationships to further improve customer focus. To achieve these objectives they decided to introduce a bonus scheme that went across sales and marketing departments. The reason for doing this is that they believed that it would encourage sales and marketing to work together and remove some of the conflicting objectives between the two groups. They introduced other motivational tools to help overcome the resistance to change, including additional training, discussion forums and seminars, etc. The organization found that they made a number of mistakes when implementing the new reward system. There was initial misunderstanding of what should be achieved and how each team should be contributing. Further, there were considerable costs of implementation in the short term. As time went on they redesigned some of these bonus schemes to make them more project based with clearly defined objectives. Overall, they did feel that the new sales and marketing behaviors that they wanted were achieved through the new reward system and the motivational training schemes that they had put into place. Further, the end result was worth the initial costs as they now had a collaborative sales and marketing team that was focused on the customer and long-term success.

Rewards Alignment

The thorny issue of appropriate rewards frequently has been raised as a method of improving collaboration between sales and marketing. Academic literature proposes that if rewards are aligned with achieving common objectives then conflict will be reduced and collaboration increased (Kotler, Rackham, and Krishnaswamy 2006; Rouzies et al. 2005). The issues that are highlighted are that differences in reward structures between functional groups can create serious coordination problems. Sales and marketing are often rewarded through different systems, and may be incentivized to achieve different objectives, for example, brand awareness (marketing) or clearing stock (sales) (Fincham and Rhodes 1999; Alldredge, Griffin, and Kotcher 1999). Being set different rewards and goals occurs even though sales and marketing are part of the same overall function that should have a single overall objective.

Prior research into the interface between marketing and R&D indicates that aligning rewards, or incentivizing staff through using the same metrics, can help the participants to take shared responsibility for achieving targets and then enjoy the rewards. Reward systems are meant to focus employees on achieving the organization's overall objectives, and therefore to be successful the rewards should be achievable, and compatible with the roles assigned, and targets set (Galbraith 2002). Further, there are areas where sales and marketing activities clearly overlap, for example, the issue of collecting market intelligence. If sales and marketing staff are to take data collection seriously then they should be briefed clearly on the objectives, measures, and rewards (Evans and Schlacter 1985). While this may not be too difficult for marketing people, sales personnel will need to achieve an appropriate balance between the time required to create sales and collect information. If there is an appropriate reward for creating market intelligence then sales and marketing staff will be able to collaborate, as they will be willing to allocate the time to the activity. Salespeople should be explicitly rewarded for using their time gathering market intelligence, or they are unlikely to give the activity sufficient attention to be successful (Festervand, Grove, and Reidenbach 1988; Grove et al. 1992).

There has been recommendations for senior managers to focus on setting "superordinate goals," to help align sales and marketing staff. This "superordinate goals" would be compelling targets that require all the resources and efforts of the combined group to be achieved. If rewards are put in place to reflect the achievement of these "superordinate goals," then collaboration can be supported and activities can be aligned (Coombs and Gomez-Mejia 1991; Hauser, Simester, and Wernerfelt 1994). Consequently, there is a move to compensate sales personnel for the achievement of "superordinate goals" such as company profits, achieving revenue targets, or successfully launching a new product offer (Kotler, Rackham, and Krishnaswamy 2006; Strahle, Spiro, and Acito 1996). Using rewards to achieve overall objectives helps to remove the barrier of individually incentivized targets. If both groups are given rewards (in whatever form) to achieve the same goals, they are more likely to be motivated to cooperate and coordinate their activities (Le Meunier-FitzHugh, Massey, and Piercy 2011).

Summary

In this chapter we have considered the tools and activities that senior management may use to align sales and marketing. Integration mechanisms (e.g., cross-functional meetings and joint planning, cross-functional teams, cross-functional training, job rotation, and reward alignment) provide a tool kit that is available to managers seeking to improve the sales and marketing interface. Although these mechanisms are individually effective, the most efficient combination for an individual organization will depend on the industry and the organization's culture and structure.

- It is essential that organizations develop processes that facilitate the alignment of sales and marketing functions.
- Cooperation and the development of people, skills, and knowledge, are essential to success.
- Rewards need to be considered when discussing sales and marketing collaboration.

The next chapter will consider the optimization of sales and marketing relationships.

Key Points

1. Senior managers should be aware of the need to signal the importance of sales and marketing collaboration.
2. There are a number of integration mechanisms that may be employed to assist with facilitating collaboration, but the circumstances of the organization and the structure of their sales and marketing operation will both influence which mechanisms are most effective.
3. Cross-functional meetings are probably the most effective integration mechanism, although to achieve buy-in from the participants these meetings should have a specific purpose and benefit both groups.
4. Job rotation is a powerful tool, but may be difficult and costly to implement.
5. Rewards may be employed to align sales and marketing activities.

CHAPTER 7

Optimizing the Sales and Marketing Interface

Introduction

Defining the most effective relationship between sales and marketing personnel has consistently presented organizations with a number of challenges. We would repeat that, on the whole marketing and sales personnel have good personal working relationships, but the demands of their roles and their interdependence creates tensions that, if unaddressed, can lead to conflict. The barriers to collaboration between sales and marketing are very real. They have developed as sales and marketing have grown into distinctive functional areas with their own culture, objectives, and infrastructure. Organizations can go some way to relieve these tensions by senior managers communicating their support for sales and marketing collaboration, and employing integration mechanisms such as team projects, joint meetings and planning sessions, job rotation, cross-functional training, and aligning rewards. There are also other ways of improving collaboration between sales and marketing, by creating a learning culture, removing barriers and encouraging positive interaction. Another area that may help with improving the sales and marketing interface in the long term that is within senior manager's control is the architecture and structure of the organization.

Structure and Process

Although traditionally organizations have been vertically structured into specialist departments or functional areas (Day 1997), there are only two basic options for sales and marketing—as a single, joint department, or as two separate departments (Biemans and Brencic 2007). Within this basic division, five different configurations of the sales and marketing functions have been identified, which relate to different levels of power, knowledge, linkages, orientation, and information sharing (Homburg, Jensen, and Krohmer 2008). Each configuration was measured for the level of sales success achieved and the two most successful were Brand-Focused Professionals and Sales-Driven Symbiosis. The conclusion is that the most effective sales and marketing configurations occur where there is a high degree of expertise held within the sales or marketing departments and that this knowledge is shared. Sharing expertise develops understanding of each other's roles and a high level of learning may be created, whether or not the dominant function is sales or marketing.

It has been argued that "successful marketing organizations will be structured around major customers and markets, not products, and will integrate sales, product strategy, distribution, and marketing communications competences and activities." (Webster 1997, 64) This statement appears to hold true and it is the organizational structure that may be configured to either facilitate or impede collaboration (Rouzies et al. 2005). Consequently, it is clear that whichever sales and marketing structure is selected for the organization it must facilitate collaboration to provide a high level of customer and market knowledge for the organization. The most effective structure of sales and marketing for each organization should be supported by process alignment, which is in turn facilitated by agreed goals and boundaries. Agreement over roles and boundaries also helps to identify accountability and performance standards between the two groups. The whole aim is to gain an understanding of each other's contribution to achieving overall strategic marketing and sales objectives. One part of the process alignment will be over the sticky issue of lead generation and the sales funnel or pipeline. This process should be seamless and each party should be clear about their roles and responsibilities (see Chapter 3). The customer should not notice any difference in their interactions with the organization, whether it is being handled by sales or by marketing. The whole process of customer management has been both facilitated and complicated, by the development of the web and social media. Who handles which type of interaction, and who is responsible for various content is open to debate. Again it is clarity over responsibilities that help to facilitate agreement (see Diagram 12).

Diagram 12 Processes where Sales and Marketing Contribute in the Customer Value Chain

Communication

The whole area of communication has provided a lively debate (see Chapter 4) over not only the most effective type and frequency of communication, but also over the forums where communication should take place. Communication frequency, formal or informal, presents a challenge. Too little and understanding is not achieved, too much time is wasted and staff become overloaded. Bidirectional information appears to be an appropriate solution, but this can be difficult to establish unless common forums can be agreed. Between marketing and sales there are a number of crossover areas where bidirectional communication can be established and fruitfully be developed, for example, market information systems, planning activities, and new product development (NPD). These activities provide areas of common interest that impact on the effectiveness of both functional areas.

The most obvious area of joint interest is over lead generation and the sales funnel as mentioned above. This may be extended into customer relationships (see Chapter 5). Traditionally it has been the sales department that has been responsible for customer management, but with the development of social media and the web, marketing has become more involved in this important activity. The result is that some organizations struggle to maintain consistent marketing messages, brand values, and processes. Consequently, some customer and consumers are receiving confused or incoherent messages and suffering poor customer service. Improving collaboration between sales and marketing can go a long way to relive this situation and this may be achieved through the development of trust.

Trust is helpful in building relationships not only between sales and marketing staff, but also between the customer and the organization (see Chapter 4). Establishing appropriate levels of interpersonal trust and interorganizational trust can also be helpful in the creation of customer value. Customers wish to interact with an organization in a manner that is acceptable and beneficial to them. As a result it is up to the sales and marketing staff (in their boundary-spanning function) to jointly establish the needs and wants of the customer and delivers the value that they require. Continuous value creation through the sales and marketing processes can ensure that the customer value chain is engaged and satisfied.

Location

Despite a move within many organizations to centralize their management systems, there are still very many sales functions that are based regionally (Day 1997). This creates a physical separation of sales and marketing staff that may be difficult to overcome. It has been suggested that locating sales and marketing staff in separate locations may prevent informal meetings and opportunities to hold discussions face to face over coffee or in the office to improve understanding (Dewsnap and Jobber 2000). This physical separation may be less critical in smaller organizations where information can be exchanged during interaction at organizational meetings, although frequent interaction may still be hard to achieve (Viswanathan and Olson 1992). It is argued that allocating office space to sales managers near to marketing managers may be one way of helping to improve the working relationship between sales and marketing (Dewsnap and Jobber 2000). However, it is unlikely that increased interaction through physical proximity is really the key to improving alignment. It is the generation of constructive dialogue that is critical to improving the sales and marketing interface and this is unlikely to be achieved through their informal interactions (Le Meunier-FitzHugh and Piercy 2008). Consequently, wherever sales are located, improving their relationship with marketing is likely to be reliant on formal interactions.

The Role of Learning in Collaborative Behavior

Organizational learning provides another stream of thought. Marketing is a cross-department, boundary-spanning function that can play a key role in establishing organizational learning. Collation and dissemination of market information is the linchpin of this role. However, the majority of functional groups will use a mixture of their own codified and non-codified language to communicate ideas with each other (Bechky 2003).

Coded language is usually underpinned by buried or tacit knowledge. Tacit knowledge is usually specific to a community and is only easily understood within that group because it is context specific. To promote organizational learning and facilitate understanding it is necessary to reduce coded language and liberate tacit knowledge. This may be achieved by providing an appropriate corporate architecture (Loermans 2002). It is possible to establish a suitable architecture for learning through creating processes for active participation and shared practices (Roberts 2006). The creation of a common understanding and language through problem sharing activities can underpin learning (Carlile 2004). The creation of a learning community should include information dissemination and the effective sharing of the interpretation of that information between the relevant groups. The ability to share expertise and discuss knowledge in an effort to solve collective problems is a fundamental exercise for collective learning (Van der Vegt and Bunderson 2005). Further, creating areas of shared experience and expertise can lead to a common language, which may form the basis of two groups to create a learning community.

Customer Value

The strength of creating a collaborative sales and marketing function is that it is a significant source of customer satisfaction. Customers emphasize that the presence of collaboration between sales and marketing enhances the interorganizational dimensions of trust. They trust the competence of the sales and marketing staff, and benefit from their goodwill. This encourages customers to commit to the supplier relationship (see Chapter 5). An additional benefit from a collaborative sales and marketing relationship is that there is an emphasis on competitor activities and this has been found to have a strong impact on business performance (Le Meunier-FitzHugh and Piercy 2007). Collecting and using information about competitors, learning about the organizations' capabilities and responding to competitor activities, helps organizations to adjust offers in a timely manner to changing market conditions, and to invest in new offers to the market (Noble, Janszen, and Wierenga 2002).

Cross-functional sales and marketing collaboration is essential to delivering excellence in the customer relationship and to customer satisfaction (Guenzi and Troilo 2007). Integrating the deep insights into the customer that may be gained from sales with the wider information and brand concepts held by marketing provides a powerhouse for design and innovation for organizations competing on the global stage. It is marketing and sales together that are the critical elements in customer insight, and designing and delivering value to customers (Capon 2011). To achieve increased sales, and to develop an effective sales force, sales managers must know what marketing is trying to achieve. Sales may also play a critical role in helping marketing to be successful. The role of marketing in internal integration is one of the less well-known tasks of marketing (Capon 2011).

Marketing should be able to pull the various functions within the organization together so that they can focus the organization's resources on creating customer value. Effective internal integration is a good practice and can enable organizations to gain the external integration necessary to win their market share. The sales force also has an important role to play in both internal and external integration, but it is only through collaboration with marketing that this role can be successfully executed.

Practical Integration

Having reviewed some of the tools that may be used to improve the sales and marketing interface (see Chapter 6), it is clear that senior management will need to use a range of diagnostics to identify how collaboration can be encouraged in their particular context. There is some evidence to indicate that marketing are acting in a more transactional manner than sales, and that sales are the people who engage with consultations with customers. While this may be true in some instances, marketing now have the opportunity to develop consultative or even relationship marketing with the customers through social media. If marketing efforts are measured in a similar way to sales (perhaps through achieving superordinate goals) then they can be rewarded in a similar manner to sales. This would remove one of the major sources of conflict between the two groups (asymmetric rewards). Alternatively, sales and marketing can be jointly measured on the development and conversion of prospective leads.

The range of activities undertaken by sales and marketing mean that there are plenty of opportunities for crossover working, for example, buyer mapping can be integrated with targeting new prospects, developing market intelligence is beneficial to both parties, and sales and marketing could engage in joint marketing planning. Cross-functional teams may be effectively employed in achieving some of these tasks. Developing marketing tools requires the understanding of what the customers are looking for and whom they should be targeting. Consequently, new content and tools are constantly changing to meet individual customer needs, and cross-functional training could facilitate this. Cross-functional training may also be employed to assist with developing a joint understanding of how sales and marketing roles interconnect and help to develop a culture of learning. Marketing is about communication and community and the development of marketing generated opportunities and consequently the creation of a buyer centric pipeline can provide the ultimate opportunity for the integration of sales and marketing activities.

Management Role

Senior management play a critical role in directing the sales and marketing relationship as they need to set cohesive goals and targets, and communicate a clear message about what they want the sales and marketing team to achieve. This requires vision and the structures and systems to support that. The vision should therefore encompass people, processes, and technology so that sales and marketing teams can achieve the sales results necessary for the organization's success. One helpful method is to encourage sales and marketing to develop the market offer together with a focus on creating customer value. It is really not possible for one function to achieve this on their own, as marketing may not have the complete picture of the competitor and customer needs, while sales can help implement marketing plans, but do not have the resources to communicate with both customers and consumers.

Marketing can develop awareness, communicate brand values, and develop channels in the market thereby helping sales to secure market share and volume over the mid to long term. By allowing sales to have input into the marketing process, and requiring marketing to respond to sales feedback. It is then possible to create a virtuous circle of collaboration.

Sales and marketing managers should focus on ensuring that the products, offers, and marketing materials are fit for purpose. There should be a clear dialogue between the two functions about what is required, how customers' needs are changing, and the types of information that customers require. This dialogue may be conducted through formal communication channels or through technological channels. Organizations should allow salespeople to do what they are best at and marketing should provide information and materials in a manner that is helpful and useful.

The integration of sales and marketing processes and alignment of objectives and targets may encourage the view that there is little difference between sales and marketing. However, it is more a case of trying to create a good marriage. People are very different, but it is possible to create a partnership, based on trust and a single overall objective. Rather like starting to date at the beginning of a relationship, it is necessary to come prepared to trade and compromise, and to know what you and they want. When you are building a relationship between sales and marketing it will take time and there may not be immediate gains. However, it is worth working at. Start with a conversation, develop understanding, and build trust, and a profitable relationship can be built to everyone's benefit (see Diagram 13).

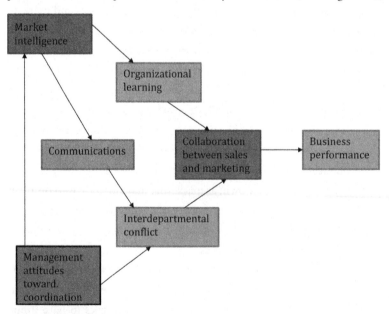

Diagram 13 *Optimizing the Sales and Marketing Interface*

Source: Le Meunier-FitzHugh and Piercy 2007.

Five Key Points in the Sales and Marketing Collaboration

The role of marketing is to understand buyers and this should drive their links to sales. The difficulty is that the personality and individuality of buyers and the development of many different sales channels, makes this complex. The challenge is to bring sales and marketing together and develop the opportunities for sales and marketing collaboration. Some of the recommendations have included both mental perspectives and practical advice:

1. "Like a football team, sales and marketing should interact, and the team should play to win." This is a good piece of advice that should be considered by all organizations with separated sales and marketing functions. The problem is—what should the sales and marketing team look like? Marketing creativity does not necessarily sell more on its own, so investments should be made in assimilating the sales perspective and creating a new team perspective of what is going to be achieved and how it can be achieved. This includes developing a joint value proposition both internally and externally. Team working is important and senior managers should be focused on developing it between the sales and marketing functions.

2. "It is all about creating and understanding customer value leading to competitive advantage.". While customer value is difficult to establish a collaborative sales and marketing team are likely to be more successful than the individual functions in meeting customer needs. Each function has something unique to contribute, but together they can really make $1 + 1 = 3$ for the customer.

3. It is important to defuse conflict and not try to avoid it. Some conflict between functions is helpful in ensuring that preconceptions are challenged, decisions discussed, and objectives are met. By bringing sales and marketing together to discuss options and solutions to joint problems and tasks it is possible to use their different perceptions of the market to create customer value. The trick is to prevent conflict from becoming dysfunctional or destructive so that collaboration is maintained and this may be achieved through communication and trust.

4. Another suggestion is to use technology to facilitate collaboration through increased communication. Technology has changed the customer and organizational landscapes, and it has the potential to do the same for the sales and marketing interface. Using appropriate communication tools enable detailed and technical communications that facilitate understanding across physical distance.

5. The creation of customer journeys helps everyone to know where they are in the sales process and may be used to create customer success stories for marketing to use in promotions. Include sales in planning for new offers and then they can sell more as they buy into the brand values being created by marketing. Understanding each other's roles and having a plan to achieve combined objectives can assist with creating collaboration.

Conclusion

The objective of this book has been to set up a debate, both internally and externally, about the operations of the sales and marketing functions. Some of you reading this book will say, "we know all of this" or "we do all of this," but hopefully this review is a useful reminder of some of the dangers of ignoring the operation of your sales and marketing functions. It is helpful to set up a dialogue about the direction that you want to take with the sales and marketing interface and consider the relevant architecture and structure to support collaboration. Is there a forum for sharing information, market intelligence, and developing a joint coded language? How is the importance of collaboration communicated to your sales and marketing staff by senior management? Most importantly do sales and marketing collaborate through areas of overlap in their operations for example, marketing intelligence, NPD, or customer management (developing new customers and existing customers)? Whichever view you take on the sales and marketing interface, the key thing to remember is that when sales and marketing work well together (collaboratively) it has been shown to positively affect, not just on profitability, but also customer satisfaction and customer retention.

References

Aaker, D.A. 2001. *Strategic Market Management*. 6th ed. New York: Wiley.

Aberdeen Group. 2002. "Bridging the Divide: Process, Technology, and the Marketing/Sales Interface." *Market Viewpoint* 15, no. 4. pp. 1–12

Aberdeen Group. 2010. "Sales and Marketing Alignment Collaboration Cooperation—Peak Performance"

Alldredge, K. G., Griffin, T. R., and Kotcher, L. K. 1999. "May the Sales Force Be with You." *McKinsey Quarterly* 3, pp. 110–21.

American Marketing Association. 2004 *"Definition of Marketing,"* http://www .google.co.uk/url?sa=t&rct=j&q=&esrc=s&source=web&cd=5&ved=0C DkQFjAE&url=http%3A%2F%2Fwww.marketingpower.com%2FAbou tAMA%2FDocuments%2FAmerican%2520Marketing%2520Associatio n%2520releases%2520new%2520Definition%2520for%2520Marketing .pdf&ei=mEriU-DNBOHC7AaHx4HYBw&usg=AFQjCNG5CjjVrH2SM-2s18Lo0mdSc2lZRQ&bvm=bv.72197243,d.ZWU, (accessed May 2004)

Anderson, J. C., and Narus, J. A.1990. "A Model of Distributor Firm and Manufacturer Firm Working Partnerships." *Journal of Marketing* 54, no. 1, pp. 42–58.

Anderson, R. E., Dubinsky, A. J., and Mehta, R. 1999. "Sales Managers: Marketing's Best Example of the Peter Principle." *Business Horizons* 42, no. 1, pp. 9–26.

Armstrong, A. G., Enright, H., Lempres, E. C., and Reuch, S. 1996. "What's Wrong with the Consumer Goods Organization". *McKinsey Quarterly* no. 1 (Winter), pp. 126–135.

Athens, D. 2002. "Integration between Marketing and Sales", *American Marketing Association*, Chicago, IL. www.marketingpower.com/live/contenet-printer-friendly.php? &Item_ID.16836 (accessed 19 March 2002).

Bals, L., Hartmann, E., and Ritter, T. 2009. "Barriers of Purchasing Departments' Involvement in Marketing Service Procurement." *Industrial Marketing Management* 38, no. 8, pp. 892–902.

Barclay, D. W. 1991. "Interdepartmental Conflict in Organizational Buying: The Impact of the Organizational Context." *Journal of Marketing Research* 28, no 2, pp. 145–59.

Baumann, J., and Le Meunier-FitzHugh, K. 2014. "Value Co-Creation and Interpersonal Trust in Customer-Salesperson Interaction—An Imperative for Transactional and Relational Exchange?" *AMS Review* 4, no. 1–2, pp. 5–20.

Becerra, M., and Gupta, A. K. 2003. "Perceived Trustworthiness within the Organization: The Moderating Impact of Communication Frequency on Trustor and Trustee Effects." *Organization Science* 14, no. 1, pp. 32–44.

Bechky, B. A. 2003. "Sharing Meaning across Occupational Communities: The Transformation of Understanding on a Production Floor." *Organization Science* 14, no. 3, pp. 312–30.

Berry, L. L. 1995. "Relationship Marketing of Services & Growing Interest, Emerging Perspectives." *Journal of the Academy of Marketing Science* 23, (Fall) no 4, pp. 236–45.

Biemans, W. G., and Brencic, M. M. 2007. "Desinging the Marketing-Sales Interface in B2B Firms." *European Journal of Marketing* 41, no. 3/4, pp. 257–73.

Biemans, W. G., Brencic, M. M., and Malshe, A. 2010. "Marketing–Sales Interface Configurations in B2B Firms." *Industrial Marketing Management* 39, no. 2, pp. 183–94.

Biggemann, S., and Buttle, F. 2009. "Coordinated Interaction and Paradox in Business Relationships." *Journal of Business and Industrial Marketing* 24, no. 8, 549–60.

Blois, K. J. 1998. "Don't All Firms Have Relationships?" *Journal of Business and Industrial Marketing* 13, no. 3, 256–70.

Capon, N. 2011. "Marketing: The Anchor for Sales." In *The Oxford Handbook of Strategic Sales and Sales Management*, eds. Cravens D., Le Meunier-FitzHugh, K., and Piercy, N. F. Oxford: Oxford University Press, 571–95.

Carlile, P. R. 2004, "Transferring, Translating, and Transforming: An Integrative Framework for Managing Knowledge Across Boundaries." *Organization Science* 15, no. 5, pp. 555–68.

Cespedes, F. V. 1995. "Coordination Sales and Marketing in Consumer Goods Firms." *Journal of Consumer Marketing* 10, no. 2, 37–55.

Child, J. 1985. *Organization: A Guide to Problems and Practice.* 2nd ed. London: Harper & Row.

Cohen, S. G. 1993. "New Approaches to Teams and Teamwork." In *Organizing for the Future*, eds. Galbraith, J. R., and Lawler, E. E., III. San Francisco, CA: Jossey-Bass. pp. 194–226.

Coombs, G., and Gómez-Mejia, L. R. 1991. "Integrating Compensation Strategies Manufacturing and R & D." *Compensation and Benefits Review*, 23, no. 5, 15–26.

Cooper R. G. 1996. "New Product: What Separates the Winners from the Losers." In *PDMA Handbook for New Product Development*, ed. Rosenau M. D., Jr. New York: John Wiley.

Cordery, J. 2002. "Team Working." In Warr, P. ed. *Psychology at Work*, 5th ed. London: Penguin Books. pp. 326–50.

Crosby, L. A., Evans, K. R., and Cowles, D. 1990. "Relationship Quality in Services Selling: An Interpersonal Influence Perspective." *Journal of Marketing* 54, no. 3, pp. 68–81.

Cross, J., Hartley, S. W., Rudelius, W., and Vassey, M. J. 2001. "Sales Force Activities and Marketing Strategies in Industrial Firms: Relationships and Implications." *Journal of Personal Selling and Sales Management* 21, no. 3, pp. 199–206.

Das, T. K., and Teng, B.-S. 2001. "Trust, Control, and Risk in Strategic Alliances: An Integrated Framework." *Organization Studies* 22, no. 2, p. 251.

Dawes, P. L., and Massey, G. R. 2005. "Antecedents of Conflict in Marketing's Cross-Functional Relationship with Sales." *European Journal of Marketing* 14, no. 11/12, pp. 1327–44.

Day, G. S. 1997. "Aligning the Organization to the Market." In *Reflections on the Future of Marketing: Practice and Education,* eds. Lehman, D. R., and Jocz, K. E. Cambridge: Marketing Science Institute, pp. 67–96.

De Dreu, C. K. W., and Weingart, L. R. 2003. "A Contingency Theory of Task Conflict and Performance in Groups and Organizational Teams." In *International Handbook of Organizational Teamwork and Cooperative Working,* eds. West, M. A., Tjosvold, D. and Smith, K. Chichester, United Kingdom: Wiley, pp. 151–66.

Dewsnap, B., and Jobber, D. 2000. "The Sales–Marketing Interface in Consumer Packaged-Goods Companies: A Conceptual Framework." *Journal of Personal Selling & Sales Management* 20, no. 2, pp. 109–19.

Dewsnap, B. and Jobber, D. 2009. "An Exploratory Study of Sales—Marketing Integrative Devices." *European Journal of Marketing* 43, no. 7/8, pp. 985–1007. doi: 10.1108/03090560910961489

Dougherty, D. 2001 "Re-Imagining the Differentiation and Integration of Work for Sustained Product Innovation." *Organization Science* 12, no. 5, pp. 612–31

Dwyer, F. R., Schurr, P. H., and Oh, S. 1987. "Developing Buyer-Seller Relationships." *Journal of Marketing* 51, no. 2, pp. 11–27.

Ernst, H., Hoyer, W. D., and Rübsaamen, C. 2010. "Sales, Marketing and R&D Cooperation across New Product Development Stages: Implications for Success." *Journal of Marketing* 74, no. 5, pp. 80–92.

Evans, K. R., and Schlacter, J. L. 1985. "The Role of Sales Managers and Salespeople in Marketing Information Systems." *Journal of Personal Selling & Sales Management* 5, no. 2, 49–55.

Festervand, T. A., Grove, S. J. and Reidenbach, R. E. 1988. "The Sales Force as a Marketing Intelligence System." *Journal of Business and Industrial Marketing* 3, no. 1, pp. 53–59.

Fincham, R., and Rhodes, P. 1999. *Principles of Organizational Behaviour.* 3rd ed. Oxford: Oxford University Press.

Fisher, R. J., Maltz, E., and Jaworski, B. J. 1997. "Enhancing Communication Between Marketing and Engineering: The Moderating Role of Relative Functional Identification." *Journal of Marketing* 61, no. 3, pp. 54–70.

Galbraith, J. R. 2002 *Designing Organizations.* San Francisco: Jossey-Bass.

George, M., Freeling, A., and Court, D. 1994. "Reinventing the Marketing Organization." *McKinsey Quarterly* no. 4, (Autumn) pp. 43–62.

Grönroos, C. 1990. "Service Management: A Management Focus for Service Competition." *International Journal of Service Industry Management* 1, no. 1, pp.6–14.

Grönroos, C. 1994. "From Marketing Mix to Relationship Marketing: Towards a Paradigm Shift in Marketing." *Management Decision* 32, no. 2, pp. 4–20.

Grönroos, C. 2011. "A Service Perspective on Business Relationships: The Value Creation, Interaction and Marketing Interface." *Industrial Marketing Management* 40, No 2 pp. 240–47.

Grove, S. J., LaForge, M. C., Knowles, P. A., and Stone, L. H. 1992. "Improving Sales Call Reporting for Better Management Decisions." *Journal of Consumer Marketing* 9, no. 4, pp. 65–72.

Guenzi, P., and Georges, L. 2010. "Interpersonal Trust in Commercial Relationships—Antecedents and Consequences of Customer Trust in the Salesperson." *European Journal of Marketing* 44, no. 1/2, pp. 114–38.

Guenzi, P., and Troilo, G. 2006. "Developing Marketing Capabilities for Customer Value Creation through Marketing-Sales Integration." *Industrial Marketing Management* 35, no. 11, pp. 974–88.

Guenzi, P., and Troilo, G. 2007. "The Joint Contribution of Marketing and Sales to the Creation of Superior Customer Value." *Journal of Business Research* 60, no. 2, pp. 98–107.

Hammer, M., and Champy, J. 1993. *Reengineering the Corporation: A Manifesto for Business Revolution.* New York: Harper Business.

Harker, M. J., and Egan, J. 2006. "The Past, Present and Future of Relationship Marketing." *Journal of Marketing Management* 22, no. 1, pp. 215–42.

Hauser, J. R., Simester, D., and Wernerfelt, B. 1994. "Customer Satisfaction Incentives." *Marketing Science* 13, no 4, pp. 327-50.

Hennig-Thurau, T., Gwinner, K. P., and Gremler, D. D. 2002. "Understanding Relationship Marketing Outcomes—An Integration of Relational Benefits and Relationship Quality." *Journal of Service Research* 4, no. 3, 230–47.

Homburg, C., and Jensen, O. 2007. "The Thought Worlds of Marketing and Sales: Which Differences Make a Difference?" *Journal of Marketing* 71, no. 3, pp. 124–42.

Homburg, C., Jensen, O., and Krohmer, H. 2008. "Configurations of Marketing and Sales: A Taxonomy." *Journal of Marketing* 72, no. 2, pp. 133–54.

Homburg C., Workman, J. O., Jr. and Jensen O. 2000. "Fundamental Changes in Marketing Organization: The Movement Towards a Customer-Focused Organizational Structure." *Journal of the Academy of Marketing Science* 28, no. 4, pp. 459–79.

Hughes, D., Le Bon, J., and Malshe, A. 2012. "The Marketing–Sales Interface at the Interface: Creating Market-Based Capabilities through Organizational Synergy." *Journal of Personal Selling & Sales Management* 32, no. 1, pp. 57–72.

Hulland, J., Nenkov, G. Y., and Barclay, D. W. 2012. "Perceived Marketing–Sales Relationship Effectiveness: A Matter of Justice." *Journal of the Academy of Marketing Science* 40, no. 3, pp. 450–67.

Ingram, Thomas N., Schwepker, C. H., Jr. and Hutson, D. 1992. "Why Salespeople Fail." *Industrial Marketing Management* 21, no. 3, pp. 225–30.

Johnson, D., and Grayson, K. 2005. "Cognitive and Affective Trust in Service Relationships." *Journal of Business Research* 58, no. 4, pp. 500–07.

Juttner, U., Christopher, M., and Baker, S. 2007. "Demand Chain Management-Integrating Marketing and Supply Chain Management." *Industrial Marketing Management* 36, no. 3, pp. 377–92.

Kahn, K. B. 1996. "Interdepartmental Integration: A Definition with Implications for Product Development Performance." *Journal of Product Innovation Management* 13, no. 2, pp. 137–51.

Kotler, P., Rackham, N., and Krishnaswamy, S. 2006. "Ending the War Between Sales and Marketing." *Harvard Business Review* 84, no. 7–8, pp. 68–78.

Krohmer, H., Homburg, G., and Workman, J. P. 2002. "Should Marketing Be Cross-Functional? Conceptual Development and International Empirical Evidence." *Journal of Business Research* 55, no. 6, 451–65.

Krol, C. 2003. "Why Can't Marketing and Sales get Along?" *BtoB Magazine*. http://www.btobonline.com/cgi-bin/article.pl?id=10833 (accessed 22 April 2002).

Lawrence, P. R., and Lorsch, J. W. 1976. *Organization and Environment.* Homewood: Richard D. Irwin,

Le Meunier-FitzHugh, K. and Piercy, N. F. 2006. "Integrating Marketing Intelligence Sources: Reconsidering the Role of the Salesforce." *International Journal of Marketing Research* 48, no. 6, pp. 699–716.

Le Meunier-FitzHugh, K. and Piercy, N. F. 2007. "Does Collaboration between Sales and Marketing Affect Business Performance?" *Journal of Personal Selling & Sales Management* 27, no. 3, pp. 207–20.

Le Meunier-FitzHugh, K., and Piercy, N. F. 2008. "The Importance of Organizational Structure for Collaboration between Sales and Marketing?" *Journal of General Management* 34, no. 1, pp. 19–36.

Le Meunier-FitzHugh, K., Massey, G. R., and Piercy, N. F. 2011. "The Impact of Aligned Rewards and Senior Manager Attitudes on Conflict and Collaboration between Sales and Marketing." *Industrial Marketing Management* 40, no. 7, pp. 1161–71.

Le Meunier-FitzHugh, K., Baumann, J., Palmer, R., and Wilson, H. 2011. "The Implications of Service-Dominant Logic and Integrated Solutions for the Sales Function." *Journal of Marketing Theory and Practice* 19, no. 4, pp. 423–40.

Leenders, M., Janszen, F., and Wierenga, B. 1994. "Structuring the Marketing–R&D Interface in Pharmaceutical Companies for Successful Innovation." Paper presented to the *EPhMRA/ESOMAR Conference on Pharmaceutical Environment: Meeting the Pressures by Intelligent Resourcing*, Lisbon, June, pp. 41–56.

Lian, P. S., and Laing, A. W. 2006. "Relationships in the Purchasing of Business to Business Professional Services: The Role of Personal Relationships." *Industrial Marketing Management* 36, no. 6, pp. 709–18.

Loermans, J. 2002. "Synergizing the Learning Organization and Knowledge Management." *Journal of Knowledge Management* 6, no. 3, pp. 285–94.

Lorge, S 1999. "Marketers are from Mars, Salespeople are from Venus." *Sales and Marketing Management* 151, no 4, pp. 27–33.

Macfarlane, H. 2003. *The Leaky Funnel*. Toorak, Australia: Bookman Media

Malshe, A. 2010. "How is Marketers' Credibility Construed within Sales-Marketing Interface?" *Journal of Business Research* 63, no. 1, pp. 13–19.

Maltz, E., and Kohli, A. K. 1996. "Market Intelligence Dissemination across Functional Boundaries." *Journal of Marketing Research* 33, no. 1, pp. 47–61.

Massey, G. R., and Kyriazis, E. 2007. "Interpersonal Trust between Marketing and R&D during New Product Development Projects." *European Journal of Marketing* 41, no. 9/10, pp. 1146–72.

Matthyssens, P., and Johnston, W. J. 2006. "Marketing and Sales: Optimization of a Neglected Relationship." *Journal of Business & Industrial Marketing* 21, no. 6, 338–45.

McAllister, D. J. 1995. "Affect- and Cognition-Based Trust as Foundations for Interpersonal Cooperation in Organizations." *Academy of Management Journal* 38, no. 1, pp. 24–59.

Macdonald, E. K., Wilson, H., Martinez, V., and Toossi, A. 2011. "Assessing Value-in-Use: A Conceptual Framework and Exploratory Study." *Industrial Marketing Management* 40, no. 5, pp. 671–82.

Moenaert, R. K., and Souder, W. E. 1990. "An Information Transfer Model for Integrating Marketing and R&D Personnel in New Product Development Projects." *Journal of Product Innovation Management* 7, no. 2, pp. 91–107.

Mohrman, S. A. 1993. "Integrating Roles and Structure in the Lateral Organization." In *Organizing for the Future,* eds. Galbraith, J. R., and Lawler, E. E., III. San Francisco: Jossey-Bass, pp. 109–93.

Moncrief, W. C., and Marshall, G. W. 2005. "The Evolution of the Seven Steps of Selling." *Industrial Marketing Management* 34, no. 1, pp. 13–22.

Mouzas, S., Henneberg, S. C., and Naudé, P. 2007. "Trust and Reliance in Business Relationships." *European Journal of Marketing* 41, no. 9/10, pp. 1016–32.

Noble, C. H., Sinha, R. K., and Kumar, A. 2002. "Market Orientation and Alternative Strategic Orientations: A Longitudinal Assessment of Performance Implications." *Journal of Marketing* 66, no. 4, pp. 25–39.

Oliva, R. A. 2006. "Three Key Linkage: Improving the Connections between Marketing and Sales." *Journal of Business and Industrial Marketing* 21, no. 6, 395–98.

Olson, E. M., Walker, O. C., Jr. and Ruekert, R. W. 1995. "Organizing for Effective New Product Development: The Moderating Role of Product Innovativeness." *Journal of Marketing* 59, no. 1, pp. 48–62.

Palmatier, R. W., Dant, R. P., Grewal, D., and Evans, K. R. 2006. "Factors Influencing the Effectiveness of Relationship Marketing: A Meta-Analysis." *Journal of Marketing* 70, no. 4, pp. 136–53.

Palmer, A. 1994. "Relationship Marketing: Back to Basics?" *Journal of Marketing Management* 10, no. 7, pp. 571–9.

Payne, A. F., Storbacka, K., and Frow, P. 2008. "Managing the Co-Creation of Value." *Journal of the Academy of Marketing Science* 36, no. 1, pp. 83–96.

Piercy, N. F. 2006. "The Strategic Sales Organization." *Marketing Review* 6, no. 1, pp. 3–28.

Piercy, N. F., and Lane, N. 2005. "Strategic Imperatives of Transformation in the Conventional Sales Organization." *Journal of Change Management* 5, no. 3, pp. 249–66.

Piercy, N., Cravens, D. W., and Lane, N. 2007. "Enhancing Salespeople's Effectiveness." *Marketing Management 16,* (September/October) pp. 17–25.

Porter, M. E. 1980. *Competitive Strategy.* New York: Free Press.

Powell, T., and Allgaier, C. 1998. "Enhancing Sales and Marketing Effectiveness Through Competitive Intelligence." *Competitive Intelligence Review* 9, no. 4, pp. 29–41.

Pralahad, C. K., and Ramaswamy, V. 2004. "Co-Creation Experiences: The Next Practice in Value Creation." *Journal of Interactive Marketing* 18, no. 3, pp. 5–14.

Roberts, J. 2006. "Limits to Communities of Practice." *Journal of Management Studies* 43, no. 3, pp. 623–39.

Rousseau, D. M., Sitkin, S. B., Burt, R. S., and Camerer, C. 1998. "Not so Different After All: A Cross-Discipline View of Trust." *Academy of Management Review* 23, no. 3, pp. 393–404.

Rouzies, D., Anderson, E., Kohli, A. K., Michaels, R. E., Weitz, B. A., and Zoltners, A. A. 2005. "Sales and Marketing Integration: A Proposed Framework." *Journal of Personal Selling & Sales Management* 15, no. 2, pp. 113–22.

Sako, M. 2002. "Does Trust Improve Business Performance?" In *Trust Within and Between Organizations*, eds. Lane, C., and Bachmann, R. Oxford: Oxford University Press, 88–117

Schmonsees, R. J. 2006. *Escaping the Black Hole: Minimizing the Damage from Marketing–Sales Disconnect*. Mason, OH: Thomson South-Western.

Shapiro, B. 2002. "Want a Happy Customer? Coordinate Sales and Marketing." Boston: Harvard Business School. http://hbswk.hbs.edu/pubitem.jhtml?id=3154&sid=0&pid =0&t=customer (accesed 12 Feb 2009)

Sheth, J. N., and Parvatiyar, A. 1995. "The Evolution of Relationship Marketing." *International Business Review* 4, no. 4, pp. 397–418.

Sheth, J. N., and Shah, R. H. 2003. "Till Death do us Part . . . but not Always: Six Antecedents to a Customer's Rrelational Preference in Buyer-Seller Exchanges." *Industrial Marketing Management* 32, no. 8, pp. 627–31.

Sheth, J. N., and Sharma, A. 2008. "The Impact of the Product to Service Shift in Industrial Markets and the Evolution of the Sales Organization." *Industrial Marketing Management* 37, no. 3, pp. 260–69.

Shultz, D. E. 1998. "Invest in Integration." *Industry Week* 247, no. 10, p. 20.

Sloane, R. 2010. *It's all Here in Black and White Alignment: The Secret to Getting Your Sales and Marketing Teams Working Together*. Oxford: Sunmakers

Strahle, W. M., Spiro, R. L., and Acito, F. 1996."Marketing and Sales: Strategic Alignment and Functional Implementation." *Journal of Personal Selling & Sales Management* 16, no. 1, pp. 1–20.

Tjosvold, D. 1988. "Cooperative and Competitive Interdependence." *Group Organization Management* 13, no. 3, pp. 274–89.

Troilo, G. 2012. "Integrating Sales and Marketing." In *Sales Management*, ed. Guenzi, P., and Geiger, S. Basingstoke: Palgrave Macmillan

Tuli, K. R., Kohli, A. K., and Bharadwaj, S. G. July 2007. "Rethinking Customer Solutions: From Product Bundles to Relational Processes." *Journal of Marketing* 71, no. 3, pp. 1–17.

Ulaga, W., and Eggert, A. 2006. "Value-Based Differentiation in Business Relationships: Gaining and Sustaining Key Supplier Status." *Journal of Marketing* 70, no. 1, pp. 119–36.

Van der Vegt, G.S., and Bunderson, J. S. 2005. "Learning and Performance in Multidisciplinary Teams: The Importance of Collective Team Identification." *Academy of Management Journal* 48, no. 3, pp. 532–47.

Vargo, S. L., and Lusch, R. F. 2004. "Evolving to a New Dominant Logic for Marketing." *Journal of Marketing* 68, no. 1, pp. 1–17.

Vargo, S. L., and Lusch, R. F. 2011. "It's all B2B...and beyond: Toward a Systems Perspective of the Market." *Industrial Marketing Management* 40, no. 2, pp. 181–7.

Viswanathan, M., and Olson, E. M. 1992. "The Implementation of Business Strategies: Implications for the Sales Function." *Journal of Personal Selling & Sales Management* 21, no. 1, pp. 45–57.

Webster, F. E., Jr. 1997. "The Future Role of Marketing in the Organization." In *Reflections on the Future of Marketing 1997, Practice and Education*, eds. Lehman, D. R., and Jocz, K. E. Cambridge: Marketing Science Institute, pp. 39–66.

Weitz, B. A., and Bradford, K. D. 1999. "Personal Selling and Sales Management: A Relationship Marketing Perspective." *Journal of the Academy of Marketing Science* 27, no. 2, pp. 241–54.

Willcock, D. I. 2013. *Collaborating for Results*. Farnham, UK: Gower Publishing.

Woodruff, R. B., and Flint, D. J. 2006. "Marketing's Service-Dominant Logic and Customer Value." In *The Service-Dominant Logic of Marketing: Dialog, Debate, and Directions*, eds. Lusch, R. F., and Vargo, S. L. New York: Sharpe.

Wright, S., Pickton, D. W., and Callow, J. 2002. "Competitive Intelligence in UK Firms: A Typology." *Marketing Intelligence and Planning* 20, no. 6, pp. 349–60.

Zaheer, A., McEvily, B., and Perrone, V. 1998. "Does Trust Matter? Exploring the Effects of Interorganizational and Interpersonal Trust on Performance." *Organization Science* 9, no. 2, pp. 141–59.

Index

OTHER TITLES IN OUR SELLING AND SALES FORCE MANAGEMENT COLLECTION

Buddy LaForge, University of Louisville and Thomas Ingram,
Colorado State University, Collection Editors

- *Sales Technology: Making the Most of Your Investment* by Nikolaos Panagopoulos
- *Effective Sales Force Automation and Customer Relationship Management: A Focus on Selection and Implementation* by Raj Agnihotri and Adam Rapp
- *Customer-Oriented Sales Management Practices: Text and Cases* by Ramendra Singh
- *Sales Force Ethical Decision Making: A Guide for Sales Professionals* by Lawrence Chonko and Fernando Jaramillo
- *Managing and Conducting Sales as a Project: Synergies Between Sales Methodologies and Project Management Techniques* by Richard Owen
- *Competitive Intelligence and the Sales Force: How to Gain Market Leadership Through Competitive Intelligence* by Joël Le Bon

Announcing the Business Expert Press Digital Library

Concise e-books business students need for classroom and research

This book can also be purchased in an e-book collection by your library as

- a one-time purchase,
- that is owned forever,
- allows for simultaneous readers,
- has no restrictions on printing, and
- can be downloaded as PDFs from within the library community.

Our digital library collections are a great solution to beat the rising cost of textbooks. E-books can be loaded into their course management systems or onto student's e-book readers. The **Business Expert Press** digital libraries are very affordable, with no obligation to buy in future years. For more information, please visit **www.businessexpertpress.com/librarians.** To set up a trial in the United States, please contact sales@businessexpertpress.com

0 1341 1487685 4

DATE DUE

RETURNED

CPSIA information can be obtained at www.ICGtesting.com
Printed in the USA
LVOW04s1431211015

459181LV00018B/986/P

9 781606 498583